God Spoke to Me Today

ISBN: 979-8-9864947-0-8   [Paperback Edition]
          979-8-9864947-1-5   [eBook Edition]

Printed and bound in The United States of America.

God Spoke to Me Today

.... and I began to listen

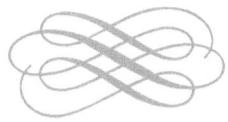

A JOURNEY THROUGH HELL TO FREEDOM

BY

PAIGE RENEE JEFFCOAT

This book is dedicated to my family for always being supportive.

To my children for forgiving me and turning into such wonderful young adults. Leigh Ann, Lauren, Savana, and Dakota! I'm proud of each one of you. You have your own path to follow and I pray that eventually that path leads you to a trusting relationship with God.

To all the ones that lost their battle to addictions or depression, there are so many, too many to name.

I pray this book leaves you with hope for a better future of knowing that life can be different, it can be good and fulfilling. All it takes is asking for help.

I would like to acknowledge The Owl's Nest Recovery Center in Florence, SC for giving me the tools I need to continue becoming a better person each day.

I would like to acknowledge my family for not disowning me when admitting my problem and supporting me through all of my troubles and through growth.

I would also like to acknowledge Newspring Church in Florence, SC and in Columbia, SC for being supportive, accepting and loving me as I was growing in God's love. I'm also grateful for Newspring Church being in my life to help guide me to a better understanding of God.

There are so many I would love to acknowledge and not nearly enough space to do so. I will say this to everyone that has crossed my path in life, thank you for your presence, whether it was a lesson for me to learn or just sharing moments of joy together. Every moment of life has made me who I am today.

Finally, the most important!

I am grateful to God, the Father, that has rescued me from the pits of hell and continues molding me into His creation and not my creation.

~~~~~~

Psalm 96:3 (NLT) Publish his glorious deeds among the nations. Tell everyone about the amazing things he does.

Ten percent of the proceeds will be placed into a non-profit account to help those in recovery or seeking recovery.

~~~~~~

I specifically chose not to have this book edited. These are my words and every one of my flaws. None of us are perfect. I could have chosen to allow the publisher to edit and have this book sound very professional, but that's not who I am. I'm just me. I'm no longer an edited version of myself. I learned that when people, like me, close ourselves off due to not knowing how to cope with life, we stop growing mentally and have difficulty communicating in words what we're feeling. I didn't begin learning how to communicate effectively until I was forty-eight and this includes learning to comprehend what others are saying, not what I think someone is saying.

I have been writing this book for three years and from the beginning to the end, I can see growth in myself from my writing. It may not be much, but I can see it. Laying down my addictions was not the end of me, but only the beginning. I'm grateful every day for things that I learn. The only way I have been able to learn is by allowing myself to accept that I am not always right and there are more perspectives in life than just mine.

A Battle of The Mind

This battle in my head is driving me insane.

Someone come save me, I wish I were dead.

I'm tired of all the lies, that you keep spinning.

I thought I was in control, but you keep winning.

This world is so cold, nobody cares at all.

I try and pick up all the pieces, but I stumble and I fall.

From deep within my soul, I'm full of love to share.

But tired of loving you, You don't even care.

I've cried out for you, please come and hold me tight.

Please come and save me, just tell me it's alright.

This battle in my head is driving me insane.

You don't need to save me, I'm already dead.

Wherefore he saith, awake thou that sleepest,
and arise from the dead, and Christ shall give thee light.

Ephesians 5:14 (KJV)

After I wrote that poem, I held a loaded 9mm under my chin, safety off, ready to end it all. I couldn't deal with the pain anymore. It wasn't just pain from not receiving love from the man I wrote this poem about, it was a lifetime of pain and not knowing what love was and not knowing how to feel loved. I was also holding onto much guilt and shame that I hadn't let go of. I only continued to pile more on top of what was already buried in me. It's like I got to a point where I could stuff nothing more into me. I was holding all of it that I could inside of me, ready to explode. It was spilling out of me, onto everyone around me and had been for years. My finger was on that trigger, I just couldn't bring myself to pull it. I realized that I didn't want to die, I just didn't want to live in the pain I was in anymore and didn't know how to cope with life. I was trying, my way, to kill the parts of me that I hated. My way of doing things, would have ended badly with yet another mess for someone else to clean up.

Usually, after writing things like this and not following through with my thoughts, I would tear them up and throw it away. I don't remember why I held onto it, but I found it about a year later and the entire meaning changed when I found it. I found it after leaving the recovery center and moving into the next phase of my life. The poem wasn't about anyone else but me. I was tired of lying to myself. I was tired of all the voices in my head telling me that I wasn't good enough, not worthy, nothing but a failure, and would never amount to anything. I was tired of not caring about myself or not loving myself. It was a battle between my body, soul, and spirit. That last line of not needing to be saved because I was already dead, well, I was spiritually dead inside. This was my cry to God.

Do you know what saved me from pulling that trigger? It was the spirit inside of me, a voice of reason and truth. It's always been there, I only tried to drown it out so I could live the way I wanted without having to listen to that persistent voice inside of me.

God saved me for a purpose, his purpose. It's through pain that God's greatest purposes can be achieved. My pain, for his purpose, bringing hope to others like me.

Before getting to God's wonderful love, grace, and mercy, I need to take you through my darkness. It was only living through the darkness that I was able to find what I was missing my entire life. Jesus walked through a 40- day storm of temptation after being baptized. Moses led the people to freedom, but it took him 40 years to find it. My storm was 40 years.

I had just turned 48 and was deep into an addiction to meth. Three years that I couldn't let this demon go. But this was not my first addiction. I struggled with alcohol for 28 years, including those three years of being addicted to meth. Honestly, I'm grateful for meth, otherwise, I'd probably still be drinking today. Alcohol was not my first addiction either and I didn't realize it until much later. My first addiction began at 8, not as an addiction, but it became one later. I'm hoping you'll see what I saw when I did a complete inventory of my life, how everything unfolded before my eyes.

I'm extremely hard-headed and it took God allowing me to go through hell to wake me up. He knew exactly how far to let me go until he opened my eyes and ears. What I've found throughout all of this is that once you've been touched by God, you cannot be untouched by God, he watches over you until you decide to wake up to truth.

This is the most difficult task that I've been given by God thus far. I'm not a published writer, yet, but I love writing and believe it is my gift from God.

I debated on where to begin, so I'm going to begin with the most terrifying night of my life, the one that led me to a life of recovering from self-destruction and being led to truth.

The Evil That Pretended to Be Light

(Please do not ever question me about these events because I didn't witness who did what, what the circumstances were, or what exactly happened)

I was living with a friend where we had no water and no electricity and we were actually ok with this at the time. Why is anyone comfortable with no electricity or water? When one is deep into an addiction and doesn't see a way out, that one's only comfort comes from the substance itself and it doesn't matter what we don't have, as long as we have the substance for comfort. We did have a generator, so I guess at times, we did have electricity. I stayed in a room at one end of his home and he stayed on the other end. I helped provide food and transportation, as I had a vehicle and a license at the time. He did his thing, I did mine. We lived in a world of meth and everyone I met was on meth. That's all I knew in those three years. I lived many different places, but this was the last one before I asked for help.

I had been painting the interior of my friend, Reign's house. (names changed for many reasons) I hadn't planned on going to his house on this particular day, but he texted me and asked if I wanted to come over. I thought he wanted me to come over and paint, but I never did any painting that day. I'm not sure how I got over there that day, because I didn't have my truck with me, it wasn't running right. The clutch was going out of it.

When I arrived over there and walked inside the house, I felt an eerie presence. I wasn't sure what it was, but it wasn't a good feeling. The only way I can describe that feeling is a feeling of death nearby. There were quite a few people over there that day. This was another place where we all did meth together, just not this day. I didn't know anyone's names that were over there and I'm grateful for that now. If anyone had drugs that day, nobody was using them. I didn't have any either. I think I stayed in the hopes of someone eventually having some meth. Yes, I know, that's horrible, but that was my life.

I ignored my intuition and stayed there anyway. The setup of the house was different from just a few days before. They had moved the band equipment into a small room and there were a couple of people in there on the drums, the mic, and the guitar. We usually hung out either on the opposite side of the house or in the main living area. I didn't give it much thought because when on meth, things changed constantly. There was one girl, that I'll call, Luna, that was on the opposite side of the house. No one else was on that side of the house that I knew of, just her. She was a raging lunatic this night, I just thought it was because she didn't have any dope. It was almost as if she were guarding that side of the house. Looking back over it, she was.

I was hanging out with the guys that were in the band room; Reign, Draconia, and Blaze. Draconia was trying to teach me how to rap. That was funny. He was telling me to just say what I felt. The only words that came out of my mouth were Chaos, Rage, Disorder. That's exactly what it felt like there, yet I stayed.

These events may not be in order because I don't remember the exact order they happened. At one point, I was talking to one of the girls that I saw there, Willow. She was nice to me. As I was talking with Willow, Luna came over and was in my face yelling and trying to entice me into fighting her. I didn't know what she was so mad about but I stood as tall as I could in my 4'11 frame to her 5'8 frame and said, "Luna, I'm not going to fight you. You've done nothing to me and I don't want to hurt you". I meant those words too. She left me alone after that. But then Reign came in and got into an argument with Luna and he began punching her. Although I didn't like Luna, I pulled Reign off of her because I cannot stand to see a man hit any woman. After that small incident, Reign and Draconia removed their phones from carefully positioned spots because they had their video on trying to capture, what I thought was Luna causing problems. It didn't make sense to me until I began writing this. They were trying to catch me on video fighting and causing problems. God was definitely with me this night, because if I had been drinking, I would have been all up in that chaos that was going on and fighting anyone and everyone. These events only made sense looking back over them. Reign was being extremely distant with me this night and didn't really talk to me. He wouldn't even show me the video that they had captured when he used to include me on everything. The video would have only shown him hitting Luna and her fighting back and me pulling Reign off of her. It wasn't long after this that Willow came up to me and told me that it was time for me to choose sides. I had no clue what she was talking about, but I said, "I choose Reign's side". Although he was being abusive to Luna and aloof with me, I thought he was my friend. After I said that, I went to take a shower because, like I said earlier, I had no running water or electricity where I was staying, only periodically. When I was drying off, I heard Willow and Draconia talking. Willow was saying, "she's a really good person". I knew they weren't talking about Luna and it had to be me because I was the only other female there. When I came out of the bathroom, Willow had a huge pipe wrench in her hands and Draconia told her that wasn't necessary. I didn't know what was going on. Then Reign yelled at me and said, "Paige, I'm tired of you telling me that you've got my back when you don't". He then handed me his wallet, his keys, and an expensive watch that he had on. He told me that I needed to follow through with my words, meaning, I needed to have his back. With what, I had no clue. No one had told me what was going on. I only knew it was something bad, I felt it. At that time, Luna was on her phone with someone, telling them that when they got there to not hurt the females there. Luna then opened the front door and left it open for whoever was coming. This is when I began to get scared. I saw what these people were capable of a week prior to this. I watched one of their friends, threaten Draconia with, brass knuckles, then a gun. I was with Luna and Reign while this was happening. Luna told me not to worry, that's what they did for fun. It wasn't my business, so I didn't get involved in it, but I should have learned from that incident to not go back around these people. Fortunately, that specific day, no one was beat, shot, or hurt and it wasn't Luna or Reign doing any of the threatening. It was someone else, that I had only met that day. I don't know his name or care to know.

This night was different, I felt it. I looked at the items in my hands and gave them back to Reign. I said I was done with this or something to that fact. Not even a minute later, Draconia pulled me to the side and said, "you need to leave NOW". Then a guy came running into the front door, out of breath. I don't know where he came from, but he had been running. He stood over on the side of the house where Luna had been guarding. They shut Luna in a room and told her to stay in there. He then stood in a military, at ease stance. He was now guarding that side of the house. I don't know why, but before I walked out of the front door, I walked up to that guy, shook his hand and said, "thank you". I had no clue who he was, but I felt like I was thanking him for sparing my life. Little did I know that was probably truth. I walked out and no one stopped me, it was very late at night. I was standing in the front yard not knowing where to go. This house was out in the middle of nowhere, surrounded by woods, and I was scared. I don't even know how to describe the fear that I felt. I didn't know what was going on and I didn't have my vehicle with me. Draconia came outside, borrowed my phone a moment, put a number in it, and told me to text a certain message to that number when I got away from the house. I had no clue where I was going. He kept telling me to leave now! I texted that number, the words he told me to text. I don't remember what those words were, but I know it was a code phrase for something. I got a response asking, "who is this?". I immediately turned my phone off. My thoughts were, "who did I just text? What did I just do?". I got to the edge of the woods, very close to the house, when I saw a vehicle flying up the driveway. I had just texted a "clean up" crew. I didn't realize it then, but I did later. I had just enough time to hide my bag of clothes and I stood behind a tree. I didn't think I could stand there long, so I laid flat on my stomach behind that tree, surrounded by bushes for what seemed like an eternity. I just watched. Two guys got out of the vehicle. I couldn't see who they were. I only knew they were male because I could hear their voices. They went in the house, closed the door, and all the lights went off.

I wanted to run. I kept hearing a voice that said, "be still". I didn't move either. My left arm was lying directly on top of an ant bed. When they began biting, I just looked down at my arm and in my head, I said, "keep on biting bitches, I'm not moving". It's amazing the things one can endure when you put your mind to it. Besides, my focus was on the house, not the biting ants. I heard noises that sounded like someone getting beat to death and I could hear a loud "gasp", like a last breath coming from someone. That's how close to the house I was. Some time passed and I saw these two guys bring out what looked like a body wrapped in a white sheet. One of the guys said, "where should we put them?". They loaded, whatever it was in the back of the vehicle, went back inside and brought out what seemed to be another body wrapped in a white sheet. Sheer terror swept over me. The guys loaded other items into the vehicle then left. A small light came on in the master bedroom. That was the only window that I could see from where I was hidden. There was a purple hue in that window that I couldn't take my eyes off of. I had a feeling that I had seen that same purple hue in a window before but couldn't place when or where. In my mind I was freaking out over what I had seen and terrified of being found. I am only writing these details because I don't know what went on in that house. I don't know names. I don't know whose bodies were brought out or where they were taken. I didn't even know if they were dead or alive. I didn't witness anything that took place there. (I did find out the next day who one of those bodies belonged to and she was very much alive, just got beat up. I still don't know her name and I'm glad that she's ok. I also found out who was still alive which was everyone in the house that I saw that night. I have no clue who the other body was. My guess is that someone else may have been beaten up and taken away, just like the one girl that they took away wrapped in a sheet that was alive, I just didn't know that until the next day.

I must have dozed off for a little while. I woke up to blue lights coming down the driveway. I was thinking that thank goodness, they'll find something and arrest these people. The cops went in and searched, came back out and just stood there talking to some of the guys that had been in the house. I heard Reign say my name to the cops. I guess it startled me because I moved my foot in the leaves making noise. The cop flashed his light over in my direction. My first thought was, "this is my way out of here". My second thought was, "I have a meth pipe on me and I don't want to get arrested". This led to a memory of what an officer told me months prior to this night that kept me very still and not moving. No officer could save me from the mess I was in at the moment. It doesn't matter what that officer said to me prior to this night, but just know that it saved my life. Luckily, the officer, this particular night, didn't see me. I was hidden better than I thought. Lying flat on the ground helped. The police left and everyone went back inside. I was still trying to figure out how to get out of this predicament. The sun was about to come up and I knew I had to make a move. I was about to make a run for it to the neighbor's house when I heard someone behind me, not sure where, but behind me clapping their hands. It sounded like they were walking up the driveway. That sent me into another state of being frozen in fear. I thought I was found for sure. I waited a few minutes and didn't move. I heard nothing. I was not about to stand up and run, so I belly crawled to the neighbor's house. Literally. I was filthy, but I didn't care. I didn't know where else to go. I left my belongings in the woods because I couldn't slide them with me as I was crawling down the driveway to his house. The neighbor let me in and let me sleep on a mattress that had been on the floor. I didn't even take my shoes off. I was so exhausted, I passed out. I'm not even sure how long I slept for. This man woke me up later and dummy me told him what I had seen the night before. He told me he was going up there to talk to them and he got into his truck and went up there. Great, now they knew I saw part of what was going on. I couldn't stay in that house anymore. I grabbed the man's loaded 22 (Interestingly, I was over at this man's house the day before, getting brand new cabinets that he was going to throw away and I was taking them to Reign's house using this man's truck. He, for some reason, showed me where he had all of his guns hidden while I was over there getting those cabinets for Reign's house) I felt bad for taking his gun, but I didn't know what was going to happen. I went out of his back door, left my phone behind and I military maneuvered my way to the hog wire fence. I kept facing where I was leaving to make sure no one was coming. I did a backwards roll over that fence, always keeping my eyes facing where I was retreating from and crawled through the woods with that gun in my hands until I got to a point where I felt safe enough to stand up and walk. I don't know how long I walked through those woods, because I couldn't get my bearings straight. I finally came to the end of the woods, near a very familiar road. I didn't want to take the gun with me, so I left it buried under some brush at the corner of the woods. I didn't think it would look very good for me to be walking down a road, carrying a loaded rifle. I could have walked to where I was staying, about 3 miles away, but I was filthy, looked horrible and needed to rest. So I walked to an ex-boyfriend's house that wasn't far. No one was home there so I sat outside waiting. I no longer had my phone to call anyone. I left my phone behind because I began to feel like those events were setting me up for taking the fall for something I had no clue of. I wanted nothing more to do with that phone. I had allowed several people to borrow it while in that house the night before. I also thought that someone put some sort of tracking device on it. I don't think anyone did, but that was the state of fear I was in. While resting in the shade, someone showed up and they took me to where I had been living. I got out of the vehicle looking like hell and there were a few people there. Again, dummy me, opened my mouth, and told them what happened. I don't think anyone believed me which is a good thing. But people talk. I stayed in that house for maybe a week after all this happened. I was terrified to go anywhere. I was afraid someone was going to come over and get me because of what I saw. The last night I stayed at this house, the guy who owned it left for the night. So I was alone and scared to death. I didn't want to stay in the house by myself, so I got a few of my things and locked myself in his shed constantly looking out the window.

I couldn't take anymore. I was finally given the gift of desperation. The next afternoon, when my roommate retuned home, I used his phone to contact my brother, Richard. I told Richard that I needed help, gave him the address and asked if he would come pick me up. This was close to dark that next day. He and his wife came and picked me up. When I got in the truck, my sister-in-law, Gina, asked me if I was using drugs. Like any addict, my first response was no. But they had to have known. My behavior had changed drastically, I was losing my mind, and I had dropped down to 95 lbs. It wasn't even a second later, that I said, "yes, I've been addicted to meth". This was the first time ever admitting to anyone that I had a problem. Once a problem is admitted, then I knew I had to seek help to resolve it. Denying a problem only kept me stuck in the problem. This was the beginning of my freedom.

I spent the night with them that first night, then Richard took me to our parents the next morning. At this point of my addiction, my skin felt like it was just rolling down my face and I was convinced that there were bugs in my skin. Psychosis from using. To this day, I deal with some of the skin sensations, sometimes wanting it to be real instead of me being "crazy".

Due to the fear that I was in, my brother suggested I go to a treatment facility for safety issues. I knew he meant for me to get help and I would have gone for that reason as well. So, three days after Richard and Gina picked me up, I was on my way to a recovery center.

〜〜〜〜〜〜〜〜〜〜〜〜〜〜〜〜〜〜〜〜〜〜〜

Psalm 96:13-17

....for your love for me is very great. You have rescued me from the depths of death. O God, insolent people rise up against me; a violent gang is trying to kill me. You mean nothing to them. But you, O Lord, are a God of compassion and mercy, slow to get angry and filled with unfailing love and faithfulness. Look down and have mercy on me. Give your strength to your servant; save me, the son of your servant. Send me a sign of your favor. Then those who hate me will be put to shame for you, O Lord, help and comfort me.

〜〜〜〜〜〜〜〜〜〜〜〜〜〜〜〜〜〜〜〜〜〜〜

God revealed these verses to me after I left the recovery center. God was showing me that he does take care of us. That's exactly how I felt that night in the woods, like they were going to kill me or they were setting me up to take the fall for their mess. Either way, it wouldn't have ended well. I prayed under that tree. God heard me. He answered and I slowly began to listen.

Willingness To Accept Help

Richard drove me to the recovery center on a Sunday morning. I was excited to go. Who gets excited about going to a recovery center?

- someone that was sick and tired of being sick and tired
- someone that was totally lost in life
- someone that needed answers to why I kept doing the things I hated doing
- someone that was finally asking for the right kind of help and accepting the help provided
- someone that kept making the same mistakes over and over again not knowing how to stop repeating them
- someone that was finally ready to heal
- someone that was finally desperate enough to ask for help

When we turned into the driveway of the facility, I told Richard, "I'm supposed to be here". He said, "yes you are" and laughed. Then I said, "no, I'm supposed to be HERE". I felt it before even seeing the property. It was beautiful. But that feeling of me knowing that I was meant to be HERE, I interpreted as for a greater purpose, so I entered this facility with a little arrogance in me. It didn't matter, I was there, and I was willing to learn. I was still exhausted from three years of not much sleep.

My first week was pretty good. At least I felt safe. Remember that purple hue I mentioned that I saw from the woods that I thought I had seen before, well I finally saw it. We were walking back to our living quarters after our retirement at night, when I looked up and saw it radiating from the window by my bed. We had purple sheer curtains and a lamp was left on which created that purple hue from the window. Yes, this was a sign from God that I was supposed to be here. There were many signs from God while I was in the treatment center. I took all of them as meaning for my greater purpose. No, it was for God's purpose to begin working on me. I initially signed up for the 28-day program. Basically, it was a 12-step boot camp. I opted to stay for 28 more days. For 56 days, I was learning about steps that I would use the rest of my life, but I didn't realize it at the time. My mind was still cloudy and things I heard didn't always sink in. I was learning, but not applying what I was learning to my life yet.

During the second week of being in the center, I was sitting in a class listening about the disease of addictions/alcoholism. I was listening but then began talking to myself in my head. I said, "Paige, you know you can never, ever have a drink again. Are you ok with that?". I had to think about that one for a few minutes. Then I said to myself, "Yes, I'm ok with that". I'll tell you something, since that day, I haven't consciously thought of putting another drink in my body. Those thoughts have unconsciously popped into my mind, but I let those thoughts go because they are no longer my thoughts. They're what I refer to as Satan's distractions and I put Satan under my feet. I cannot control my first thought, but I can control the ones after. Ironically, when talking to myself about never drinking again, I didn't say that about drugs. God knows every decision we're going to make before we even have a clue. This comes later in my story.

At the end of the first 15 days with no visitors, I had just come back from Newspring church (Florence, SC) and was waiting for Richard and Gina to come visit. They were my first visitors. I will never forget Gina's expression when I walked around the corner to meet them. She cried. She couldn't believe how much I had changed in 15 days. I couldn't see it, but she did. We had a good visit. She told me that I was glowing.

At some point during my stay in the recovery center, we were in a meeting and for some reason, I don't even know why, but I stated that I was going to be working with special needs children. Well, actually, I do know why I stated that, I had applied for a job with a special needs facility and honestly thought I was supposed to have that job. It didn't work out that way, but I felt that I was supposed to work with special needs. This comes at a later date in my journey with God.

While enrolled in the program, I did what I was told, for the most part, and tried my best to learn things that I was being taught. I'm grateful for this program because it not only saved my life, but also changed it. I can tell you that anyone that chooses to go to a recovery center, don't judge what you think should be different, just accept what it is and learn from it. Don't judge others because you're all battling your own demons. You will only get out of the program what you put into it. If you're judging and criticizing everything, nothing new will be able to get into your mind for you to learn how to be different. Learning all of these new aspects of coping skills was only half of the solution. The other half was practicing what I was learning.

Between June and July 2018 I was baptized at Newspring church in Florence, SC. I had been Christened as a baby and gone through confirmation classes in the church I grew up in, but I had never been baptized under water and I felt I needed to do that.

〰〰〰〰〰〰〰〰〰〰〰〰〰〰〰〰〰〰

Acts 2:38

And Peter said to them, "Repent and be baptized every one of you in the name of Jesus Christ for the forgiveness of your sins, and you will receive the gift of the Holy Spirit".

〰〰〰〰〰〰〰〰〰〰〰〰〰〰〰〰〰〰

At this point in recovery, I didn't know how deep my sins were, but I was repenting of them. God revealed them to me later.

My Guidelines For A Better Way Of Living

- Admitted that I was powerless over alcohol/drugs, my thoughts, and my life. I had created an entire mess of my life trying to do things my way.
- Accepting that I am not God and I have no control over anyone else's actions or words or how someone chooses to live.
- Accepting that life just "is" and being true to myself and to God.
- Came to believe that God could restore me to who he originally created me to be.
- Made the decision that I couldn't, but God could, so I turned my life over to his care.
- Wrote out an entire life history of my resentments, fears, and harms that I caused to others. I wrote mine in chronological order, this made it easy to see why I did things the way I did.
- Admitted my life's wrongs to another human being and God, repented of my sinful nature and asked for forgiveness.
- Became willing to ask God to remove my sinful nature from me.
- Humbly asked God to remove sinful defects of thinking and actions towards others.
- Made a list of all persons that I needed to make amends with.
- Began making amends with these people, if possible, except when making an amend might cause harm to that person or another.
- Continue to evaluate my life every night and repenting, when necessary, as to not place myself within that prison of my mind again.
- Began praying and meditating. Building a relationship with God as I understood him. Praying and giving him my problems, concerns, and worries and waiting for a response from God, if any.

- Began sharing my testimony of how living by God's word has restored my life and continue learning to live a life that is true to me and God. Helping others, helps self.

Living Sober Outside Of A Recovery Center

I graduated this program in August 2018 and stayed with my parents that weekend. But I didn't feel safe staying home, I still had some fear in me from what I saw before asking for help. l had a huge fear of people finding me and wanting to kill me. So I did life backwards. My mom got me an apartment in Florence, SC, close to the recovery center. I had an apartment before I had a job, so I was still relying on my parents for support. What I should have done was gone to a sober living home after the recovery center. Life would have been easier. I learned a lot through my mistakes that first year. I had gotten a 3-bedroom apartment because 2 of the girls at the recovery center had promised me that they were going to help me with the apartment after they graduated the program at the end of that week. This never happened. I allowed people to move in with me that had gotten kicked out of the recovery center because they had no where to go and I couldn't stand to see anyone on the streets. I had each and every one of them sign a contract that if they used or drank while living there, that they would be asked to leave without notice and would have to leave immediately. Every one of them relapsed and had to go. It was sad, but that's when I realized that I cannot save anyone. What really opened my eyes is one of the girls asked to use my phone to text her boyfriend in a different state. Prior to her using my phone, I had asked the girls staying with me if they would like to join me in daily devotionals and studying about recovery. They all agreed and seemed to want to do that. People will tell you what they think you want to hear in order to get what they want. I know, I did that for years. It wasn't until this particular girl gave me my phone back after using it, that I saw truth. She didn't delete her messages and she was telling her boyfriend that I was making them listen to devotionals and she couldn't stand it. This hurt my feelings a little, and

I got mad about the text message, but never said anything to her about it. I just brushed it off. I didn't make them do anything. I only asked. They agreed, then complained about it to others. I laugh now, because I did those types of things all of my life. Agreeing to something that I didn't like just to get what I wanted and then complaining about what I had agreed to do to everyone else outside of the situation.

After I followed through with and staying true to my word in the agreement of the living arrangement, I had to ask everyone to leave, at different times. One of them I had a hard time getting to leave. During this time, I had met a guy on facebook that seemed lost and depressed in life. I reached out to him because I could relate to everything he was saying. I noticed that he had gone through the same recovery center two years prior, that I had just gotten out of. I offered him a place of sobriety, a place for him to recover, and a room of his own. This is how blind I still was. I heard him ask me if he could bring his girlfriend with him. I remember this because I told him that the only way she could come was if she were clean and sober and willing to stay that way. Do you believe that I forgot about this the very next day because of the conversations he and I had? I got so lost in our conversations, false reality, that I had completely forgotten that he even had a girlfriend. I got caught up in lies.

I was 3 months clean and sober and this guy wasn't even 24 hours sober, although he told me that he wasn't drinking. I had just been lecturing others about not getting into a relationship early in sobriety and I was falling into my judgements of others fast. This guy, I'll call him Matt, got on a bus in Greenville just a few days after I began chatting with him and moved into my apartment. My only intention was to give him a sober place to get better. The events that followed were repeated behaviors that I had yet to see in myself. When I picked him up from the bus station, he reeked of alcohol, second ignored red flag. I wasn't happy at all about that, but he was already here in Florence now and I felt responsible for him because I convinced him to come to Florence. I gave him his own room in the apartment, but he didn't stay in there long. He was in my room very quickly. We became intimate before truly getting to know each other. I talked about God and the bible a lot. I also talked about recovery a lot.

Those were my main conversations, nothing else. Matt got irritated with me about it. He wanted to do things, like go to movies, bowling, whatever it was. For me, I wasn't interested in any of that at the time because I was going through a process of recovering and learning about myself. I wanted to attend meetings, continue going to church and work on me. I was boring for sure, but that was necessary for my recovery and growth. Matt had no interest in going to meetings, changing his ways, going to church, nothing. His defiance against recovery truly bothered me. He and I talked about recovery a lot before he got on that bus. He seemed to really want to recover from his addictions, but when he got settled in the apartment with me, his true colors came out. Sure, he may have wanted to be sober and as far as I could tell, he stayed sober, just without working a program of recovery. He only wanted to go out and have fun. We honestly didn't have the money for all the extra stuff anyway. After about 3 months into this relationship, of sorts, I knew that I couldn't be with him and I discussed it with him. He would accuse me of talking to other men online, and I would tell him that I wasn't. But you know what I realized later? I was talking to men, but it was about recovery. I denied talking to men because in my mind, Matt was accusing me of cheating on him or looking for someone else. I had not learned what total truth was yet. I wasn't cheating or flirting with any man online or offline for that matter, so in my mind, I wasn't actually talking to men. Does that make sense? In reality, what I told him was a lie, not an intentional lie, but a lie still the same. I wasn't trying to hurt him. I was telling him that I needed to focus on me and my recovery. I tried many times to convince him that he needed help and to get a sponsor. I tried many times to get him to go to meetings, he went to a few, but he was so closed off that he wasn't allowing himself to connect with others. He continued living in the mindset that no one understood him or how he felt. That's probably true because he wouldn't share with me how he felt about anything. I told him that he could stay at the apartment but had to stay in his own room. He didn't want to do that and told me that he was moving out at the end of the week to his own place. Since he was moving out, or so he said he was, I agreed to let someone else move into that room. Well, this became utter chaos because at the end of the week, Matt didn't move out and this new guy took over the room I had promised him. I found out later, that Matt wouldn't leave because he thought the guy moving into the room that he was moving out of, was moving in to be with me. Ya'll, I had no interest in that guy. Honestly, my interest was in making sure the rent was paid, the electric bill was paid and that I was following through with a promise to allow the new guy to move in. I should have enforced what Matt told me and I should have made him move out. Instead, I allowed him to play on my feelings and I got right back into a relationship with him. Looking back on it, I don't think he had ever talked with anyone about moving into another place, I think he only said that to spark a reaction out of me. I can tell you that if this were the case, he didn't get the reaction he wanted from me. I knew this behavior well, because I used it in the past all the time.

At this time, there were 5 of us living in a 3 bedroom apartment. A female friend, I had given her my room, the new guy, Matt, and Matt's friend in the other room. Yes, this was chaos that I allowed to happen because I didn't like hurting people's feelings so I did what I did best and wasn't true to myself, only trying to please and accommodate everyone else. The other motive? To make sure bills were paid. I wasn't working and needed them to pay the rent. It seems like I was taking advantage of them, but it worked out for all of us. They had a place to stay, very cheaply, I might add, and all their rent together covered the monthly rent and electric bill. Or, maybe that's just me justifying myself. I had always been co-dependent on others helping me with bills, especially dependent on my parents, my entire life.

I put others before myself most of the time. The biggest problem is that I didn't like conflict so I agreed with everything just to avoid a conflict, whether it was right or wrong didn't matter to me as long as I didn't have to confront anything, I was fine. This is not a good way to live. It teaches people that they can run all over you. So we lived like this for about a month. The guy that had just moved in, moved out after a month. I don't blame him. I felt bad about the entire situation but I didn't know how to stand up to others, especially when I knew the outcome was going to be ugly towards me. Then after he moved out, the girl that I gave up my room to had relapsed and I had to ask her to leave. I didn't like doing that because she was my friend, but having a signed contract made these situations easier than just telling someone they had to go because they relapsed. So, I had my room back, Matt had his room back and the other guy got to keep his room. The end of December 2018, five months out of the recovery center, I met a lady named Keri. She had just gotten out of the recovery center where I had gone. Ironically, her sister worked with our family business. I had never known that the girl from the office had a sister. I didn't ask either. Anyway, when I met Keri, I thought it was to help her, which I did in some ways, but she helped me more. I felt like I was falling, spiritually, and I was. One day I was talking with Keri about how I felt and at that moment I realized that I needed to do my rewrite my life inventory. My first attempt on writing this inventory was weak at best. I remember telling my first sponsor that I didn't have many resentments or fears. This moral inventory is about past fears, past resentments, past harms. We're to write these out to be able to see our life in front of us, to examine it, to see why we did things the way we did, to learn from it and to begin doing things differently.

I had asked Keri to be my new sponsor. I told her that I needed to do this life inventory again. I felt it, but had no clue what God was about to reveal to me in this inventory of my life.

Admitting my problem was easy for me to accept at this point of my life. I always believed in God but didn't understand what everything meant. I didn't need to understand, I only needed to surrender to God. The understanding came much later. God only gives us bits and pieces of understanding and wisdom because our minds would not be able to grasp or handle all of it at once. Besides, if God showed us everything now, we would have no reason to strengthen our faith or find dependence in him alone.

I was attending Newspring Church in Florence. It was the first Sunday of the year (2019) and the pastor's first time preaching there after his training. I took my friend, Keri with me because she had never been. I'll never forget that Sunday morning either. As we were waiting for the service to begin, I told Keri that I felt God's presence there that morning. She laughed at me. I said, "no, I really do". I don't remember what the sermon was about, but I remember the end of the service very well. Clayton King was visiting there that morning and at the end of the service he got on the stage and said that he felt God's presence there during the service. He said he didn't feel it in the earlier service, but he felt it very strongly during this service. I looked at Keri and said, "see, I told you". I don't remember Clayton King's words, but 38 of us rededicated or dedicated our lives to God that morning. I was one of them. I was taking action into proclaiming that I was giving my life to God. But, was I truly surrendering my life to God?

When I returned home, I was looking over what I had written down on my resentments and I said to myself that I still wasn't doing this right. So I prayed over my evaluation of my life and asked God to show me how he saw me. For the next 7 days all I did was work on that evaluation, from the time I woke up until I decided to go to bed. The things that came out of me were insane.

Well, I had to get the insanity out first before God could begin to be restore my mind.

Are you ready to dive into how a sick addict mind begins? Actually, one doesn't have to be an addict for their minds to be sick. This is a mind's thinking without God's presence and guidance.

A Moral Inventory of My Entire Life
A Walk Through Darkness

(I tried to write and explain at the same time)

Now to dive into this inventory that I put in chronological order from as far back as I could remember. Alcohol and drugs were never the problem, they were only temporary solutions to a much deeper problem and only an alcoholic/addict can find it in themselves by doing this inventory of their lives. To begin to resolve a problem, you must get to the root of it and dig it up. Face it and let it go.

I guess I should begin with a little background about me. I was born in May of 1970 on the outskirts of a very small town, in South Carolina. I have two wonderful parents, that are still married and both still alive today. For that, I'm truly grateful. I am the middle child and only daughter of three. We grew up in the country. The road we lived on had only 4 houses on it separated by fields for crop and/or hogs and cows. It was our house, a field, my aunt and uncle's house, a field, and my grandparents behind them. Across the street from our house was where my great grandmother lived.

We grew up going to church every Sunday. I never understood this because we didn't discuss God or Jesus in our home, ever. So, I had no understanding of God whatsoever. I don't blame anyone for this except for myself. I could have asked about God. I could have searched for him and learned about him, but I didn't. I accept that this was just how we lived. I thought God was at church, in a building, and nowhere else. Or maybe I just thought God was a part of history, I honestly didn't know. Church, from my perspective, was a place to dress up and go to and be on our best behavior. Any other time, me and my brothers were not always well behaved. We fought and argued about things that truly didn't matter. Church was a place to hear history lessons about the bible.

Our parents taught us the value of a dollar from a very early age. We planted a garden every year, as well as a huge field of peanuts. Our grandfather would plow the fields for us and we would hand plant the garden and the field of peanuts. Then we would pick the vegetables and shell peas and butterbeans, shuck corn, pull up the peanuts and pick them off the vines. We even had a couple of apple trees, peach trees, and pear trees. We were paid for doing chores around the house and for helping in the garden or the field. Some summers, we would go to my mom's brother's to pick tomatoes from his fields so he could take them to the market. I can't say that I didn't whine and complain a lot of times about doing these things but I'm grateful for learning how to grow my own vegetables, if I ever choose to and learning that it takes work to keep a garden well.

Our parents may not have given us everything we wanted in life, as in material things we selfishly wanted, but they provided what we needed, and then some.

Our mom made sure that we were well rounded and so we traveled. They took us to the World's fair in Knoxville, TN when we were young. We went to Florida a few times. We traveled to Washington DC and quite a few other places. My mom loves history so she made sure we were learning and seeing our history. We went on many vacations that others may not have had the opportunity to go on. Life is not about material possessions, its about the experiences.

Our parents also encouraged us to be involved in sports, music, dance(well me in dance, not my brothers), whatever we liked, they encouraged. I took dance lessons when I was young, tap and ballet. I didn't like ballet at all and actually had a resentment against my mom for that. Why? Because I felt awkward and embarrassed by how I did ballet and blamed my mom, not to her face, but in my head. It wasn't until years later, after recovery, that I was talking to her about the ballet. She told me that I was the one that wanted to take ballet, she didn't make me. This changed my perspective on it and then I remembered the truth and not the lie I convinced myself of. I did want to take ballet. I thought it was graceful and beautiful and I wanted to be like a ballerina. But I wasn't. I wasn't graceful at all. I became embarrassed by how awkward I felt and probably how I looked by this and instead of stating how I felt, I blamed my mom for making me take this class. I took tap lessons as well. I loved tap dancing and thought I was very good at it. I'll never forget one of the last classes I took and the last recital I was in. During class, the instructor had me and another girl, Claudia (yes, I still remember her name) tapping in the front of the classroom, in unison. The instructor was determining who was going to be the lead in the recital. Claudia was chosen and this upset me because in my mind, I tapped just as well as she did. After the tap recital, trophies were given out and of course Claudia received one, but not me. I got mad over this but didn't tell anyone about how I felt, I only stuffed those feelings. I also took piano lessons for years, but because I didn't practice much, I wasn't all that great. I could play reading music but I wasn't graceful on the piano, like others.

My perception of my mom was skewed. She was different from other moms, so I was always comparing her to others. I held onto resentments of wanting my mom to be different than she was. I wanted a loving and doting mother. What I have is a strong independent mother. She didn't show affection. I never learned how to show affection properly because I didn't learn it through experience. Everything I've learned in recovery has come from my past failures and looking at the patterns of behavior that I repeated. I had to learn to step out of the patterns and begin practicing new behaviors.

Addictions, Lies, False Reality

My first addiction began around the age of 8. I was introduced to porn magazines and became very intrigued with them. I wanted to be just like the women in the magazines. I didn't have much access to this material until a little later in life. It was forum stories, magazines, vhs movies, then later the internet. Let me be very specific. THERE IS NO LOVE IN PORN. It is only pure lust and sexual acts. You will never find love by trying to reproduce these acts in your own sexual life.

By 5th grade, we had changed schools to a community where we did not live. This was difficult for me because it was hard for me to make friends. Although, it was only 15 miles between our home and the school we attended, back then it seemed like 100 miles. I felt like an outsider at church and school because at church, I no longer attended the same school as the kids at church. Then when at school, I wasn't involved in their community events and such because we had our own things in our community. It was a different county, a different atmosphere, just different. I didn't notice until years later, but the biggest difference between the town I grew up in and the town where I graduated school from was the families. In the town I grew up in, most of the parents were still married and still are today. In fifth grade, I met many kids with divorced parents. That was a new concept to me. I didn't give it too much thought then but was well aware of many divorced parents.

I believe it was 7th grade that I began playing the clarinet in school. I was pretty good on that. I guess it was because we had band class every day at school, or maybe it was just a couple of times a week, regardless, that was the only place I could practice. I was in the band until 11th grade. I chose not to be in the band my senior year. Another girl and I competed over who would have first chair for clarinet section all the time. We seemed to rotate 1st and 2nd chair. I was ok with this.

I went through what I call a very ugly stage in life. I wasn't very pretty to say the least. All the girls in 7th grade began to have boyfriends and again, I felt unwanted. Looking back on it, there were 3 guys that liked me, but I didn't like them. I was judging their looks. Honestly, they all turned out to be very good-looking men later in life. I was the one with the problem. I was very vain and I wasn't even that cute then. I remember later in high school, after two of those guys looks changed, I wanted to date either of them. But you know what? They were no longer interested in me and had moved on. Which at that age, I really didn't need a boyfriend. I already had a lot of problems in my life that I refused to deal with. I only stuffed everything. Or if I talked about things and I didn't hear what I wanted to hear, I would get mad and stuff those feelings as well. It was never the solution I wanted for my problems, although I truly didn't know what I wanted to resolve any problem. So, I continued to pile anger on top of anger because life didn't go my way.

I used to spend time with a girl from church. This was around the age of 14. I considered her a friend. She would tell me and some of the other girls that hung out together that she didn't like this guy or that guy. But if one of us mentioned that we thought a guy was cute or we liked that guy, the ones she had just said that she didn't like, she would be all over them and would end up "going steady with them". This used to piss me off all the time. I thought that she was just taking someone from me. Well to be honest, those guys didn't like me anyway, so she wasn't taking anyone from me at all and no person belongs to another, so she couldn't take anything that didn't belong to me. At this same age, I had a small group of friends at school. Christmas was coming up and I was excited to be able to buy them a small gift to give them before Christmas break. I always thought that I gave just to make others happy without expecting anything in return. Doing this inventory and looking back on my life, this small circumstance taught me otherwise. The last day of school before Christmas break, I gave my friends their gift. They exchanged gifts with each other, but none of them, not a single one, had a gift for me. I never forgot that day because it broke my heart. I felt like I was so underserving of friends and that I wasn't loved or even liked by others. I felt I wasn't worthy enough of a small gift. I felt like this all the time in school because I was an outsider.

I debated on putting this in my book, but I need to share so you will understand where my anger came from. 7th grade was the worst year of my life, EVER. (this is by no means to harm anyone, just my story to share) I suffered from sexual trauma at this age and didn't know how to deal with it. Although none of it was my fault or my doing, I felt guilt and shame. It wouldn't be until a few years later that I talked to my mom about it, but her solution isn't what I wanted to hear. She suggested counseling and told me that I had to let it go. How could I possibly let something go that caused me so much pain and anger??? I didn't understand then. This trauma, coupled with my growing addiction to porn, perverted my view of men and love drastically. Holding on to this pain only tormented me for years and years. My anger grew into rage. All I wanted was comfort for my pain and this began my journey of looking for comfort from men, places, things to satisfy the pain, emptiness inside of me. This is important. Not long after this trauma, I felt God calling me. I didn't understand this calling at all. I talked with a couple of my friends about it, but I didn't discuss this with the right people. I understand the calling now. God was calling me to forgive. I had two responses to his calling. My first response was that I acknowledged that I heard the call, although I didn't understand it then. My second response was to walk away from God because I was angry with many people and very angry with God. Why would a loving God allow people suffer trauma that they don't deserve? Instead of forgiving the trauma and following God, I walked straight onto a path into hell. Forgiveness doesn't mean that what someone does to you is right. It only means that you are freeing yourself from the rage that will build and keep you captive until you do forgive. I found peace through forgiveness, but that was much later in life.

I met my first love at the age of 15. It was at a school dance. I fell head over heals for this guy. He was 17. I thought he and I would get married after high school. We probably would have, had I not done something really stupid. At the age of 17, my family and I took a trip to

Europe. We went to visit my older brother in Germany. He was in the Airforce and that's where he was stationed. We went to Germany, Austria, Switzerland, and France. It was an amazing trip and lots of comical events. I have to share some of our trip with you.

We rented a van to travel because there were 6 of us. Our parents, my two brothers and my cousin went with us. She was like a sister to me at the time. Richard, the one in the Airforce, was the only one with an international license, so he drove everywhere. One of the hotels we stayed in while in Berlin, I think, was under construction. There were people there and we didn't speak German and they didn't speak English. They allowed us to stay the night there in three different hotel rooms. To this day, we don't know if they were actually open for business or if the construction crew made money off of us staying there. My cousin Carla and I stayed in a room together. We were fixing our hair and putting on makeup. She sat on the edge of the sink, and the sink came off of the wall. Thank goodness the pipe didn't burst. It was hilarious. Before leaving Germany to our next destination, my brother was backing up in this rented van and hit a lamp post breaking one of the taillights on the van. Oh well, no big deal, he would get it fixed before turning the van back in. I don't remember what vicinity we were in, but Richard was driving down a cobblestone street, or maybe an alley, that had walls on both sides. We didn't think the van would fit through there, but he tried anyway. Scraped both sides of the van. So now we had a busted taillight and scrapes down the sides of the van. One night we waited too long to find a hotel so all six of us slept in that van. Not very comfortable, but we made it through the night. We got to experience going to the top of the Eiffel Tower, going to the Louvre, Notre Dame Cathedral, many places that I'm grateful for having the opportunity to visit. When we arrived back in Germany (or we could have been somewhere else, I don't remember) our mom was telling Richard to turn left at the next light because she wanted to tour the church she saw. Well Richard was not in the turning lane but was listening to mama to turn, so he did, right into a vehicle coming towards us. So, we're sitting there waiting for the police and the guy in the other car was furious and probably cursing in German. It was a brand new car he was driving. The police arrive and they're working things out. While still in the van, we notice cars surrounding another car at the stoplight where we wrecked. It was crazy. We found out that the lady driving had stolen her exe's vehicle and someone spotted it because they recognized the dry cleaning hanging in the back seat and of course recognized the car, so these people got together and surrounded her so she couldn't flee. May not be accurate details, but what I remember. We had fun, we had adventure, and experienced things that I wouldn't change.

We visited the Eiffel tower, the Louvre, Notre Dame Cathedral, saw the Berlin Wall before it was torn down, just an exciting trip that I have mostly good memories of now.

The last night we were there, Richard took me, Carla, and Rusty, my younger brother to a bar. There was not legal drinking age in Germany so we drank. I was flirting with this guy, I'll never forget his name, James, and he asked me if I wanted to walk to the park with him. He was an American soldier stationed over there. I was naïve. Richard had warned me and Carla about the guys there before we went in, but I wasn't listening to him. I should have. James ended up raping me, because even though I said "no" quite a few times, I just finally let him do whatever because I didn't know if he would get violent or not. When we got back to the bar, I was bragging to my cousin, Carla, that I had sex with this guy. Why would I brag about it? Because of guilt and shame from it. It was easier to deny what really happened and easier to tell my version of what happened. Besides, it would have meant that what Richard warned us about was true and I hadn't listened. I wasn't about to admit that someone was right about anything.

So now, back to my first love. When we returned home from our trip, he was waiting for me at the airport. I was sooooo happy to see him! I had become very dependent on him for my happiness. Too dependent. I'm sure I probably drove him crazy by not wanting him to have time away from me. I don't know how long after we returned from Germany but it couldn't have been more than a few days, I went to see him and he was extremely mad at me. I couldn't imagine what I had done to make him so mad. We had just seen each other and were happy. There it was, truth being brought into the light. He had contacted an STD from me, that I didn't even know I had. It was from the rape in Germany. So, instead of being honest with him about it, I blamed him for cheating on me. I didn't know why I lied until I listed this on my 4th step. I lied because if I had told the truth about the rape, I would have had to tell the absolute truth. The truth of me flirting with this guy all night long. That is a form of cheating. If I were so in love, why would I have given any other guy any attention? Because I made life about me and my wants. I never thought things through. I only acted on impulsive thoughts. I didn't think there would be any repercussions from hiding the truth of that night. The truth always comes to light in some way and it came to light in the form of an STD.

So instead of facing the entire truth and allowing him to make a decision based on truth and facts, I allowed him to believe what he wanted to believe, put the blame on him, and let him walk away, crushing my heart. That is the only time I can remember being so devastatingly heart broken and it was all because I did something I shouldn't have done. Put myself into a situation I didn't know how to get out of, and lied about all of it, losing the love of my life. After this, I closed my heart to love. I may have said I loved, but I couldn't possibly because I was closed off to it.

This leads us to my how I met my first husband. I went to visit my first love at his apartment but he wasn't there. I was a senior in high school at this time and I don't remember how much time had passed between our break-up and me going to talk with him.

Well, he wasn't home, but his roommate was and I actually stayed and began talking with him. In the back of my mind, I was waiting for my first love to get there, not having a clue when he might even be home. I was wanting to finally be honest with my ex about the entire situation, but instead, I fell into temptation with attention from another male.

Somehow, the roommate and I began dating. I don't remember who asked who out, but honestly, I probably asked him. I say that because I know what my intentions were behind dating him. I was hoping to make my first love jealous and get him back. Well, I got so deep into a relationship with Bryan, that I didn't know how to get out of it. He drank a lot back then. I knew it. I hated it. Even after we planned on getting married, a few days before our wedding, I threatened him. I told him that if he didn't quit drinking, I wasn't going to marry him. I did anyway. The wedding day was horrible for me. I knew at this point that I didn't want to get married, but everything was in motion and a lot of money was spent on this. My mom even came to me that day when I was getting ready and told me that I could back out if I wanted to. She must have seen how I was feeling. But, I married him anyway. I thought marriage would fix all of our issues and he would stop drinking. If there are things that someone does before you marry and you don't like those things, either accept them or let the person go. Marriage doesn't fix any of those things, it just makes it worse.

It was a fairly big church wedding. The best man in the wedding? My first love. I can't remember if I actually shed tears during the ceremony, but my heart was crying. As the minister was talking, I kept telling myself that I could still say "no". I could still back out. But I married him anyway. Why didn't I follow my heart and mind? Because of the embarrassment I would have felt for backing out of this marriage, during the ceremony. For the pain or embarrassment that I would have caused Bryan. I just couldn't do it. I have no clue what he was feeling or thinking during this ceremony. We told each other that we loved each other, but it wasn't shown in our actions towards each other. Our honeymoon? I chose to go to Disney World because I wanted to have fun. I haven't ever been the romantic type. It was a complete disaster. It rained the entire time. It didn't just rain, it came down in sheets of rain. Many of the exhibits were closed due to this. In the hotel room, a picture fell off of the wall from above the bed and hit me in the head. You think someone was trying to get my attention? I do. God was knocking me in the head to wake up from my delusional thinking. It didn't work. Then when we went to the ATM, the machine took Bryan's card and wouldn't give it back. It was not a very good beginning to a marriage. It only got worse from there. I hated his drinking. He would leave me home a lot by myself so he could drink with friends to the bars or their houses and I never knew where he was. We didn't have cell phones back then. He would take weekend fishing trips without me. Maybe not many, but he did. I have no clue what he did on those trips and don't want to know. I wasn't very nice though. I would bitch about his drinking all the time. I would get mad, yell and scream. But to others, we put on a front that everything was fine, when in reality it was never fine and only getting worse. I had heard by one of my co-workers, that they saw my husband at a bar without his wedding ring on talking to females. This was maybe at 3 months into marriage. My bright idea was to stop taking the pill at six months of marriage thinking that a baby would help bring us together. There were a couple of times early in my pregnancy, that I thought Bryan may have been cheating on me, so what did I do? Cheated on him. Honestly, that was just an excuse for me to have an affair. I wasn't getting the attention I thought I needed and found it elsewhere. Also it was my way of being vengeful. I wanted him to feel the way I felt, whether he cheated or not. I confessed later because the guilt was eating me up. Ya'll, a baby never helps a struggling marriage, only puts more stress on it. The only times I could get Bryan to help with our first daughter, were around friends. They never saw what went on at home. To some of our friends it may have looked like I did nothing and he did everything. I did get lazy during some of those times due to depression. Two years after our first daughter was born, we had another beautiful daughter. I was trying to work, had our girls in daycare, and Bryan was currently out of work. It was rough. I think I kicked him out when our youngest was about 4 or 5 months old. I was done with it all. I didn't realize how hard it was going to be trying to raise two girls, battling depression and had never learned how to be on my own. I had gone straight from my parent's home, to being married. I cannot say that the entire relationship was bad because we did have fun together sometimes. I had no clue about responsibilities and such. I became extremely overwhelmed and hid a lot of feelings and stress. I didn't ask for help. If I did ask for help, it wasn't for the right reasons. When Bryan would get the girls for the weekend, I began seeking comfort in what I hated Bryan doing, drinking alcohol. I also found temporary comfort from men. My life spiraled out of control.

The more often I drank and spent time with men, the more this behavior infiltrated our home with the girls present. I didn't drink at home, but I had men in and out of the house because I was trying to fill a void and when I didn't have alcohol, it was men that filled that void. I didn't even think about the danger I was putting my children in by having unknown men in and out of the home.

Then one night I was at a bar in Columbia. I saw a very good-looking guy standing against the wall. He was with his buddies from the army. They were stationed at Ft. Jackson. Kevin was his name. He was smart, had a good head on his shoulders, worked hard, and was very responsible. Then there I came. Bringing total devastation and destruction to Kevin's life. It wasn't intentional, I just didn't know how to handle all the things I had bottled up. I didn't know how to talk about my true feelings. I didn't know how to ask for help. Kevin stayed at my house with the girls present before my divorce was final. I was served with papers one day to appear in court for a custody hearing. I was livid! How dare Bryan try and take my kids away. Yes, at that point, I called them mine. Everything was always about me. I couldn't see how Bryan had changed for the better. He had a good job, a nice apartment, and was being responsible. I was still holding onto all the horrible things from our marriage. While he was getting better in life, I was only getting worse. I just couldn't see it. I lost custody of the girls to him. I never showed any emotion upon the court's decision, never showed any emotion when he came and picked the girls up for transfer of custody and didn't show any emotion after everyone was gone from the house that day. I had learned to completely shut off my feelings. To others, it may have looked as if I didn't care, but I did. That was the only way I knew how to survive through life was to shut off my feelings, so I didn't have to feel them. But do you know what I did with those feelings? My mind began placing blame on Kevin because he was at my house with the children present. I began blaming him for me losing custody of my girls. Not to his face, just in my thoughts. I never talked with anyone about how I was feeling, I only wanted to blame others to take the guilt from me. It was easier to blame anyone instead of looking at myself for my failures and faults. Kevin and I got married. He was a really great guy. Because I already had a drinking problem, I found myself doing to him what Bryan did to me that I resented Bryan for. Going out drinking, not telling Kevin where I was or what I was doing and leaving him home. I didn't drink all the time, but when I did, I couldn't stop until I was in oblivion. Kevin had to pick me up from the hospital one night after I had been drinking all night because I passed out in a bar's bathroom and no one could wake me up so they called an ambulance. I had alcohol poisoning. That was embarrassing, but that's what I did.

There was something I resented Kevin for, that I hadn't shared with him yet. I used to be a topless dancer for a short time. I thought this was a way to earn some quick money. I ended up spending more money on alcohol than I did on bills and providing for my children. This was one of the reasons I didn't fight for custody in court. When I was on stage one night, a man was there and was asking me questions. I didn't realize until later that this was a private investigator. I was being followed to build a case against me for a change of custody. I gave them a lot to grant that change of custody too. I didn't fight, because I didn't want all of that brought up in court.

Anyway, I had bragged about my short-lived topless dancing to Kevin when we first met. When we married, he told me that if that's what I wanted to do, it wouldn't bother him. I didn't go back to that then though. It upset me, that a man I married, would allow me to do something that was very demeaning and being stared at by other men. Instead of me telling him how I felt about that, I just added it to the things I was already blaming him for in my mind. We were not even married a year and I become a total bitch to him. I told him he had to leave. I couldn't do it anymore. I never told him why. I just wanted him gone. He left, unwillingly, but left. I know I hurt him badly, but I had no love for myself and I was only bringing disaster to him and I couldn't stand it. I hated myself. I hated blaming him for me losing custody of my children. I hated everything about me. So I did what I did best, pushed him away from me. I didn't deserve the love he had for me. That's how I felt. That hate just kept pouring over onto everyone around me. The last time I saw him was in 1994 or 1995. I don't remember. I didn't see him, talk to him, had no clue where he was. My feelings for him, I just turned off. I could turn them on and off as I felt I needed to. I felt like I was protecting myself from being hurt. I was the one causing all the pain.

Kevin had purchased a new car for me while we were married. A new Mitsubishi Eclipse. I was working for a computer company as a computer technician, so I would have been able to make the payments on this car, but I chose to spend money on alcohol instead. I bring this up because when I made him leave, he allowed me to keep the car, but I ruined his credit by not paying for it. I was irresponsible with everything. Kevin will show up in my story later in 2018.

So, I'm single again and drinking more and more because that's just how I survived. Still working for the computer firm, but began allowing my drinking to interfere with work. I ended up going back to topless dancing at night because I got a lot of attention from men there. To go on stage, I had to drink quite a bit to be able to do something that I knew was wrong. Well guess who I met there? Husband number 3.

I had not learned anything about myself or anything about what love truly meant. I was still holding onto every resentment, shame, guilt, fear that I ever had. Taking all of this baggage into yet another relationship. We were both very toxic for each other. He drank a lot, I drank a lot. I left him at one point before we got married but found out I was pregnant with our daughter. The thought never occurred to me that I could have a child without getting married. So we got married when I was about 3 months pregnant. This relationship was just doomed from the beginning. Three months after our daughter was born, I was pregnant again. This was child number 4 for me and his 4th child as well. He had two from a previous marriage. There were times when we had all 6 children in our home together, his two children, my first two children and our two children. This was very overwhelming. But it was never for any long period of time. I heard that he had been cheating on me with a co-worker, true or not I don't know, but I kicked him out when our youngest, our son, was 3 months old. Pretty much the same scenario as my first marriage. Except I brought something different into this marriage. I brought rage with me. Anytime I would get mad, I became violent and would throw things, slam things, threaten constantly. I repeated the same mistakes expecting different results. I got so mad at him that when our children were not quite 2 and 1, I packed our things up and moved me and the children to Washington State, with no money, no support system, nothing. I was moving as far away from him as possible. I found a job, had the children in daycare, and had a place to live, with a guy (imagine that) I had met online. So, honestly, I was moving for the guy, not really any other reason. I was doing ok and so were the children. It wasn't even a month after I moved there that I was stopped by a police officer. He came to the window of my car and asked me if I was Paige Forrester, that was my name at the time. I affirmed that I was. He then told me that I didn't need to pick my children up from daycare because they were in temporary protective custody and he handed me some court papers to appear in court in Washington State. My heart dropped. My first thoughts were how my babies must be scared and wondering where their mommy was. Then I was furious. Again, I couldn't see my faults. I went to court and when I heard the judge say that they were going to charge me with kidnapping, my heart fell into my stomach. If I remember correctly, they dropped the charges or suspended a 6-month jail sentence. I had no other choice but to hand over custody of our children to him. He had the children and let me see them before he put them in the car and came back to SC. This took me to another level of drinking binges and leaving the guy I was with. He used his credit to get us a place together and I ruined yet another person's credit by not being able to follow through with my promises to help. I'm not sure how much time had passed after losing custody of yet another set of children, but I received papers from my 1st ex-husband stating that they wanted his wife to adopt our girls. I had not seen them in a year, I had not paid child support like I was supposed to, I had not done anything right in life. I had just lost custody of my babies and I gave up. I didn't even fight it. I had no more fight in me. I was across the U.S. with no hope and nothing to give anyone. I knew that it was in the best interest for our girls for their step-mom to adopt them. I know they never understood that. I was extremely sick for a very long time. It's a spiritual sickness. Lost and blind in total darkness.

After about a year of drinking and losing another job (basically quitting before I got fired), I saw a sign for the military. I went and talked to an enlisting officer and took the ASVAB. I scored very high and they wanted me to go to officer's school when I enlisted. I had not yet signed any documents when I received a phone call from my mother. She informed me that a guy I had met before going to Washington State was trying to contact me. We had dated for a short time before he had to go to Korea for a year. So I called him. He wanted me to go to Texas to see him. So what did I do? Sold the car, got on a bus and went to Texas. When I got off of the bus, the first thing this guy said to me was, "you've gained weight". Yes, I had gained weight, but not the nicest thing to say to anyone. He didn't like that I had gained weight and let that be known immediately. So I'm now in Texas, had sold the car, and felt stuck so I began thinking about the military again. I went to the enlisting office there and enlisted in the Navy. I left from San Antonio, Texas in 1999 to go to Great Lakes, IL for training. I was 29 at the time. I thought the military would straighten my life out. I was excited about this but also a little scared. I was planning on going to Pensacola, FL after training for school in aviation electronics. That would have been cool. Evidently, God had other plans for me. I broke my pelvic bone during battlestations, a week before graduation. I had already been set back two weeks in my training due to shin splints. So, another failure added to all my others. I came home Christmas Eve, 1999, back to South Carolina. I had gained quite a bit of weight while in WA state and then in boot camp. My self-esteem was at an all-time low.

I had not seen my youngest children in over a year and had not seen my older children in probably two years, that led to several years before I saw my older children again. In my mind, their step-mom had adopted them, I had no rights to them, I didn't want to put myself back in their life, knowing that I would eventually fail again, because that's all I knew, failure. I remember the first time going to visit my youngest children. I believe it was around Christmas or after of 1999 that I first went to see them. My son had no clue who I was. He had just turned one when their father obtained custody, and at this time, he was two. My daughter knew who I was, she was two when her father gained custody, now three when I saw her. It was very difficult seeing my children for supervised visitation, but I did. Then I was able to have them on the weekends. It was difficult taking them back to their father after having them for a weekend. I hated it. I never showed my children how I felt though. I thought that would make them feel worse about having to go to their dads. There was one time in particular, I'll never forget. I took Savana and Dakota (that's their names) back to their dad's and Dakota was clinging to my leg, crying and begging me not to leave. Savana wouldn't let me go. That was the most difficult moment of not showing any emotion in my life and I had to let them go. Now I know another reason I needed to write this. For those emotions to finally come out. I buried them far too long. This is for my healing. I loved all of my children but didn't have any love to give.

Then I met my who was to become my 5th husband. I don't even remember what year I met him, maybe mid 2000. My drinking began spiraling out of control, yet again. He was an awesome drummer, singer, and fun to be around for the most part. We dated on and off for about 3 years. During that first year we dated, there was a group of us that hung out together. One night in particular, we were all out a local bar. Somehow, everyone left except me and a guy. I was wasted this night. I don't remember a lot about it, except bits and pieces. He and I went to Columbia to hang out in five points. When leaving there, I began to black out while driving. I was a blackout drunk, but this night I had taken a Xanax bar, first time ever taking Xanax. That doesn't go well with alcohol either. Somehow he got me to pull over and he drove. I woke up to him punching me in the face. I got out of the truck and tried to run. This guy, a friend, beat me from head to toe that night. Ripped my shirt and bra off. Tried his best to rape me but my shorts were too tight. Thank goodness for tight shorts! He had a girlfriend, I had a boyfriend. We should have not been hanging out together like we were.

The guy kept apologizing to me and I took him home. I didn't know where he lived so he was giving me directions. He took me down a dirt road and threatened me to pull over. The beating began again. I don't know why I didn't just leave him. He apologized again and I did take him to his house. So, I drove to my boyfriend's house after and told him what happened. He gave me a shirt to put on. I'm not sure if he believed me or not, but I was bruised from head to toe, two black eyes and was bleeding from the back of my head. My truck had blood on the outside of it and on the seats. After I got a shirt from him, I went to where my family's tax office was at the time. My younger brother asked me who did that to me and I wouldn't tell him because he probably would have killed that guy. I finally went to the police station and made a report. They took pictures of every bruise on my body. It was a lot. I pressed charges.

You want to know what I did? I blamed this guy for everything. I never admitted my part in it at all. Did I have a part? Oh yes, I definitely did. You see, all night long, after our friends left, this guy and I were all over each other, literally. People told me some things that I did that I had no clue that I did due to being totally wasted. I didn't deserve being beaten, but I should have taken responsibility for myself and my actions. Being totally wasted removes all inhibitions and you don't even think about anything at all. I lied to all of our friends about me having any part at all in it.

I left that relationship because he was all over the guy's (the one that beat me up) girlfriend and feeling sorry for her. He and I weren't really together though. That was me just trying to force a relationship with him. I was not a good person during these years. I was totally lost in life.

That year became very fuzzy to me and I can't remember everything or the order they happened. I do know that some time I went to Boston, MA to create a website for a company. That was pretty cool. I left there and went back to Washington State, again. I was running from myself, but wherever you go, there you are. I cannot remember how long I was there, but I was in a bad accident while working one day. I was in the median on I-5 waiting to make a left turn when I was rear ended by a lady that had a heart attack behind the wheel. I can honestly say that at least I wasn't drinking, I didn't drink while working. My truck was a total loss. My passenger that I was training, had a huge gash on her head. I had to wear a neck brace for a short time and went to physical therapy. I could tell you other events that happened in Washington, but they're not that significant. Just me doing the same things over and over again. So, I took a bus from Washington State to SC. That was a horrible trip, but I made it back. I began working as a bartender in a small hole in the wall bar and met a guy on a Sunday and married him the following Sunday in the bar. That was just insanity at it's best. We were drunk the entire time. Living in the back of the bar. I moved he and myself to my parent's house. We were not together but about 3 months. I hate admitting this next part. I went to the bar one night and ran in to the guy I had dated before going to WA state, I'll call him Anthony. I told him I had gotten married. He didn't like that. Do you know what I did? I went to my parent's house, picked up my then husband and told him that he had to leave. I drove him to his parent's house, dropped him off there and then I went to Anthony's house and stayed there. It wasn't a day or so later that my mom called me and told me that my 4th husband's parents had brought him back to their house. I wanted to leave that problem with them. I don't remember if I actually did anything about it or if they did. By this time in my life, I was totally oblivious to what I was doing and didn't care. I had cut off all feelings about anyone or anything. Sometime during that year, we were out late and my younger brother and I got into an argument at some bar. When this Anthony and I left we argued about what had happened. I was upset and angry. I opened the car door and said I was just going to jump out. Anthony told me to shut the door and he sped up to about 80 mph on a dirt road, then he told me, "if you want to jump out, jump out now". I decided I would stay in the car. Anthony lost control of the car but regained control....for a minute. Then he ran off the road and the first tree we hit, at about 80mph, we leveled with the ground. The 2nd tree we hit, we uprooted. This was a small car and it hit the tree dead center of the car. The engine was pretty much in the dash, the steering wheel was bent down, my fingerprints were imbedded in the dash and both of our heads smashed the windshield. Looking at the car and the mess, we both should have been dead or seriously injured. God was with us. We walked away without a scratch on either of us.

After I divorced my 4th husband, Anthony and I got married, in church. We stayed together 3 years. I forced Anthony to fight for custody of his children because of some things that were going on. He was awarded custody of his children and I raised them for 2 ½ years. I felt horrible because it probably looked to my younger children that I treated my step-children better than I treated my own. I may have. I felt like it wasn't my place to punish my step kids, but I would punish my own. So I could see how they would interpret my actions. Later, I realized that Anthony never wanted custody of his children. He actually tried telling me that before I forced him to take it to court. I wasn't listening to him, I was only thinking about his kids. Some of my actions could have been related to me losing custody of my own children.

We were out one night drinking. I was dancing and having fun, he was shooting pool. When I got ready to leave, he wasn't. So I left and went home and changed my shoes. My feet were killing me and blisters had already formed on my toes from wearing heals. Anyway, I went back to the bar to see if Anthony was ready to leave. I got jumped on walking into that bar, telling me I wasn't allowed there. I kept trying to tell these people that I had been there all night and all I wanted to do was talk to my husband. They forced me out of the bar. Not just one or two people, but a group. Although I had caused no problems at all on this particular night, they made me look like a problem by forcing me out and I made myself the problem by responding in anger. I was irate. Why would they act that way towards me? Because of an I got into an argument outside of this bar the weekend before. When Anthony came outside, he blamed me for everything and was yelling at me. He was raging by this point. He got in the driver's seat and I was in the passenger's seat headed home. He wouldn't stop yelling and blaming me for everything, so I punched him in the face, he hit me back. Then he told me to get out of my car, leaving me on the side of the ride to walk. I ended up getting arrested that night for criminal domestic violence and had a restraining order against me. I didn't realize how hard I had hit him until I saw the damage. It wasn't pretty. Nasty bruised eye and lip, from one punch. I guess you don't know your own strength when you're full of rage. We ended up talking and I went back home not long after this. I went through pre-trial intervention because this was a first charge. I was ordered to go through anger management classes. The first class I went to I was angry because I didn't think I needed to be there. After accepting that I had to go to these classes, I began to like them and actually learned a lot, but I didn't apply what I learned very often.

I wanted Anthony to stop drinking and I wanted to stop drinking but neither of us seemed to be able to do that. I left in the middle of the night one night. I was done. This was 2006.

Nothing I did ever lasted over 3 years. No job, (not continuous anyway), no relationship, no residency, nothing. I couldn't be still. If I were still too long I had to listen to my thoughts and I didn't like that. My thoughts would tell me where I was wrong, all the things that I had done that were wrong and I wasn't about to listen to them. My thoughts beat me down to nothing.

I'm not even sure what I did between 2006 and 2009. I drank a lot, that I know. Thankfully, I had not repeated the pattern of getting married so quickly and irrationally.

I believe that it was 2010 that I regained custody of my younger children. I was living, with yet another guy. He was a pretty good guy when he was sober. I wasn't drinking as much during this time. No, I hadn't learned my lesson yet, another toxic relationship. After I regained custody of my kids, I'm not sure how long I stayed with him because he began talking to my son, well anyone for that matter, in a negative way. He would call people stupid or ridicule them, I guess to make himself feel better than others. Anyway, I rented a house next to my parents. Then the cycles of behaviors started all over again. The men in and out, the drinking. Another difficult thing to admit, leaving my children at home by themselves while I was out getting wasted. They were 11 and 12 at that time. Maybe a little older or a year younger. My time frame is vague at best. Then we moved to Pelion to rent a trailer there so my kids could go to Pelion Schools. I found a nice little house in a nice little subdivision and my parents financed it for me. I was never a good mother. I was always drinking after work, coming home drunk. Leaving my kids to fend for themselves. I was ok when I wasn't drinking. It just seemed that my drinking was more often than not. I didn't like drinking at home and because I didn't actually drink in front of my children, I didn't see the problem. I didn't want to see the problem. My behaviors led to my daughter getting pregnant at 16, married at 17 and moved out of our home. Honestly, I don't blame her. I couldn't stand to be with myself, how could anyone else possible stand to be around me? That's why I drank. I hated me.

My daughter had moved out and my son was still living with me. I was already bad, but things went totally out of control after that. June 23, 2014 I was going to a bar to drink and shoot pool and I ran into a guy (always a guy right?) that I had met back in 2000, on my 30th birthday is when I met him. The only reason I know this exact date is because it popped up on my memory line on facebook today, as I'm typing this. My post said, "ran into a blast from the past". We picked right back up where we left off 14 years earlier. We had fun together in the beginning. Then I found out that he was using meth. I broke it off with him. I wasn't going to be around it. (Somewhere during this time, I sent my son to live with his dad because, he was growing out of my control. I couldn't control myself, much less my children.

For almost 3 months, this guy begged me back. He swore to me that he had a good job now and that he had quit the meth. So…..I took him back. It wasn't long after that I found out he was still using. I was mad. But, I had been using cocaine on and off and he pointed that out to me. What was the difference? So, on his birthday, April 2015, I decided to try meth. That was the worst mistake I ever made. From day one, I couldn't put that stuff down. Meth grabbed a hold of me and wouldn't let me go. I had a house, but moved in with my boyfriend and his mom, leaving my house empty. I tried renting it to two people, but they didn't pay rent on time and when they did, I spent that money on meth. I eventually talked my parents into owner-financing it to my friend's daughter. I basically gave away my house to use dope. I didn't need the house anymore right? My children had moved out. That was how I used to think. Just insane! By this point in my life, I had a lifetime of baggage that I had carried from one relationship to another and anything that was said to me in a negative way, I reacted in violence if I were drinking. I was a raging alcoholic. This relationship was full of my anger and me punching him and acting irate at everything! Interestingly, meth calmed me down, unless I did too much. Not long after that, my older brother had to fire me from the family business. I understood that completely. I wasn't showing up for work. I was lying about my drinking. I surely didn't tell them about my drug use. I told one of the worst lies to my family to cover my drug use. I told them I had MS, Multiple Sclerosis. That lie grew way out of control. So for the next 2 years, I moved from house to house, sleeping on couches, in spare rooms, wherever I could find, just to use drugs so my family wouldn't find out. I managed to work here and there, long enough to get gas, food, cigarettes, etc. A couple of jobs I never got paid for, and probably never will because I worked for people that were using meth. They were legitimate jobs, but I know where their money went that they made, the same place mine did, on the drug.

June or July 2017

I decided to go to Washington State to help my youngest daughter. She was now living there with her now ex-husband as he was in the military stationed there in Washington State.

I knew I couldn't help her, I was using this as an excuse to get away from South Carolina. I convinced a friend to go with me. I sold my car and we took his car. He had always wanted to go to Seattle and where my daughter was living was not too far from Seattle, so he agreed. I never told him how much money I had or how little I had. I led him to believe that I could rent an apartment when we got there. By the time we made it to Washington state, I barely had enough money to stay in a hotel overnight. Lucky for him, he knew someone in Seattle and stayed with them temporarily. I slept in his car for about a week. I was no help to my daughter. I was a mess. I ended up getting kicked out of my friend's car because he overstayed his welcome with his friends. He needed his car to sleep in and I was left to fend for myself on the streets. Well, I did it to myself. I slept on the sidewalks for about a month in Seattle. There was a nice police officer that followed me around. He was watching over me (an angel from God). He knew the people very well on the streets. He even warned me about a couple of them that I was talking to. One night he and his partner picked me up and took me to another town. They were taking me to a shelter, but when we got there, no one was there, so one of the officer's paid for a night at the hotel for me. That was above and beyond duty. I was grateful. But I ended up walking back to where I had been hanging around because I had become familiar with the area and knew where to sleep and eat. I met some very good homeless people that helped me find my way around and some even let me borrow a blanket. Although this was during the summer, the nights got really cold. I don't know why, but I never was really scared walking the streets by myself. I did run into drug users and used meth a couple of times with them. I did what I always did though. I called my family to bail me out, once again, for a predicament that I had gotten myself into. I was on a plane the next day, returning to SC. I don't know how they allowed me on that plane. My license was expired and I had a knife on me that they confiscated, but they let me on the plane. God was watching over me everywhere I went in life.

So, here I was, back in SC again. I went right back to the same type of friends and the same old drugs. It wasn't always the same friends, but we were all pretty much the same, lost in life and addicted to something. This must have been around August 2017. A lot happened between 2017 and 2018. I can't even remember it all. That's when I began hanging around with the totally wrong people. Not all drug users are bad people. The ones that I was around that last year using were not good. Some of them were actual Satan worshipers. I didn't believe that even when they told me that. I didn't think that people actually worshiped Satan, but they do exist. I found that out the hard way. This is the year that I found the rosary in Augusta, GA. This is the year that I began hearing God, but didn't quite know that it was God. I heard lots of voices, mine, God's, Satan's. I was slowly waking up to the spiritual realm. I saw some of the spiritual realm this last year during active addiction, mostly evil. I walked right into the pit of hell by continuing to do the same things in life, expecting it to "be different this time". It was me repeating the same sins over and over getting better at the sin and not knowing how to get out of it. So many times I asked myself why I did the things that I did although I didn't want to do them.

It seemed like that last six months was longer than it was. I thought it was years that had passed, but it had only been a few months between being around halfway decent people to being where I didn't belong.

AND this life path is what led me to Reign. We all read the bible together. But Reign (from the beginning of my book) would try and twist what the bible said. Reign told me he had opened the door to black magic years ago. I told him that he needed to close that door. I didn't recognize this then, but I know it now. He kept me around for a reason. People would just show up out of nowhere that we didn't know. They all said the same thing, they didn't know how they ended up there. Well, he said he didn't know them, I know I didn't know them. Many didn't hang around long. They were not naïve like I was. Reign was using my light to bring people to his house. Trying to turn people to sell their souls to the devil, just as he had. He talked about that stuff all the time. He talked about a beacon shining bright from his house that attracted people to come over. I didn't realize he was talking about me. You may not believe in a spiritual realm, but trust me, it exists. I began waking up to it after I met Reign. He saw things well before I did. He knew the spiritual realm well. I had God with me all of my life, I just couldn't see him or recognize God. Reign saw God's light in me too. I can look back and see where he was with me through everything trying to wake me up. Do you know who else knows the bible? Satan. I thought Reign was just full of crap. I found out differently.

Interesting that I gave him the name Reign for the purpose of my book. I will never mention his other name aloud again. He thought he was a god. He tried to convince me that we are all our own god. He said that he worshipped Satan and God. I told him that you can't worship both, you have to worship one or the other. He asked me why he couldn't serve both. I don't remember if I answered that question or not. He had all kinds of Satanic material around his house that he wanted me to read, I never did. After writing that last part, I looked up Satanic rituals and occults, boy was I shocked while reading it about the sexual acts they performed and how they used drugs to control others. Reign had a large dog kennel in his room that he told me he would dress women up in little girl clothes and keep them in that cage. I never saw those acts so I didn't believe it. But he did have lots of little girl's clothes and all kinds of seductive clothing for women. He never did those things to me. He also told me about all kinds of sexual acts he was involved in, I didn't care to hear about them, but he told me anyway. He told me many things that I was too naïve to believe in. After reading how the occult entices people to join, I believe everything Reign ever told me. It was like he changed from one person to another over a 6 month period. He went from having a fairly clean house to it being totally disgusting and people in and out constantly. It wasn't like that when I first started hanging out with him. He was always telling me that he was weak because he had exerted too much power when doing something. I wasn't sure what he meant by that, but he would meditate to rejuvenate himself, which is also a part of the occult. There are many religious acts with the occult, but different than Christian beliefs. I cannot believe how blind I was. I saw it all, heard it all, knew what was going on when introduced to higher ups, and still didn't believe it, because I didn't want to. I was under the belief that there is good in everyone. I don't believe that anymore. I'm not sure if he's always been this way or if something changed to lead him to the occult. It wasn't even a week before I went to his house, the night that I felt death there, that he told me he was going through initiation for a group. He even told me what that initiation meant, that he had to kill someone. Red flags everywhere!! It is my understanding that a sacrifice has to be willing, in their free will, to go where the ritual is to take place. I was willing to go over there that night. I didn't think twice about what I had been told the week prior about him going through initiation, I had completely forgotten about it.

Reign was a master manipulator. When I began to see it, I even said something to him about it. He just laughed. He would make up these crazy stories and make you believe them and have you on some kind of hunt for something all day long. I fell for that for awhile. He is also a shapeshifter. If you've never seen one, you don't want to either. I was cleaning his house for him one day before all this other evil began going on, or should I say before I began to notice it. I didn't mind cleaning actually. He started to become demanding that day, and as I'm typing this, I finally see it. He wanted me to dress in a skimpy maid uniform and I told him no. I told him that I didn't mind cleaning and it was fun, until he treated me that way, it wasn't fun and games anymore. I kid you not, his face changed into every man that ever laid a hand on me. It wasn't long after that, I left. I went back the next day because I thought maybe I had just been seeing things. He asked me why I left without saying anything to him the day before. I told him that I saw his face shift like it did. You know what his response was? "I'm sorry I did that". Who says things like that? Most people would respond with, "you're crazy!" or "You need to get off of the drugs!". Now I can look back over all of this and see that he was, what they call, "grooming" me. I didn't fall into that and he knew he couldn't control me. He knew that God had me, although I didn't even know how close God was to me then. But he tried his hardest to get me over to his side. I ignored every single warning from the very first day of ever walking into that house. Why did I ignore them? Because we used drugs together. That's the only reason I can think of. I didn't have many friends and he would always let me go over there and use with him. Usually because I'm the one that had the drugs.

There's just too much that I saw out there that was real and pure evil. If you believe in God and all of his goodness, you need to believe in Satan and all that is evil. It's never been about people against people, but only a spiritual battle. It's the spirits within us that are fighting against each other. That's why the bible states that Christians should be around other Christians. If someone doesn't want to hear about the word of God and the truth of Jesus Christ, then leave them alone because they can catch you in a snare before you realize it, by using God's word, but for their purpose, Satan's ministry, to devour your souls.

The first time I ever stepped foot into Reign's house was weird. I will briefly describe the feeling. I was visiting Reign and needed to use the restroom. When I got to that bathroom, I had the eeriest feeling in there. It wasn't just that room, but the bedroom next to it. That room was to be his daughter's room. There was one time that a female was over there with her dogs, and the dogs would not cross the threshold to go into that bedroom. It was just an eerie presence in that room. That was probably sometime in late 2017. There was something that happened a few years later that I cannot go into detail about, but it involved that little girl. I've had feelings like these throughout life, but didn't understand them and usually ignored them. I pray for all the ones still lost in the darkness, even the ones that caused harm to me or were going to cause harm to me. They are suffering and don't understand why. Why would I pray for someone that I thought was going to kill me? God tells me to. He says to pray for our enemies. I pray for Reign because he is lost in total darkness and lives in that darkness. I cannot bring him into the light, he has to be willing to come into the light. I only pray that one day he will come to God's light and love. He is still a human being. It doesn't matter what he did or didn't do, God created him, just as God created me.

Fears

I had many fears. One of my oldest fears that lingered with me for a long time was a fear of the dark. It was because I couldn't see in the dark. Wow, and there it is right in front of me. When you live in total darkness, lies, false reality, you cannot see yourself for who you truly are. You only believe the things you think you are, not actually looking at your own actions, reactions, or paying attention to any of your thoughts, only acting on them. You deny what others say about you because you just cannot see it for being blinded by the darkness in your life.

I was afraid because I didn't know what was in the dark that could bring harm to me. After leaving the recovery center, I found that It was the darkness inside of me that I was afraid of looking at. I'm the one that caused most of the harms to myself and others. I fed the sinful nature, instead of God's Holy Spirit. That sin grew and controlled me until I was 49. Some of it I still do not see, until I see it, but God has worked so much out of me in the past 3 years. It's just amazing what God can do when you allow him to. The following scripture opened my to eyes to why I continued to do things that I hated doing, but repeatedly did them anyway.

Romans 7:14-20

So the trouble is not with the law, for it is spiritual and good. The trouble is with me, for I am all too human, a slave to sin. I don't really understand myself, for I want to do what is right, but I don't do it. Instead, I do what I hate. But if I know that what I am doing is wrong, this shows that I agree that the law is good. So I am not the one doing wrong: it is sin living in me that does it. And I know that nothing good lives in me, that is, in my sinful nature. I want to do what is right, but I can't. I want to do what is good, but I don't. I don't want to do what is wrong, but I do it anyway. But if I do what I don't want to do, I am not really the one doing it: it is sin living in me that does it.

In early the part of 2017 or maybe 2018, I was living in a trailer with a female friend. It was at the end of a dirt road and beautiful huge trees. It had to be during the spring/summer because it was hot outside. At the bottom of the hill was a friend of our's mobile home. It was pitch black down there and I didn't like it. During the time that we stayed there, not long, I decided that I was going to begin facing my fear of the dark. I would walk to the bottom of the hill, to the double wide at night with a flashlight and turn around and turn my flashlight off and begin walking up the hill. It was pitch black because the trees blocked out any light. There was a tiny beam of light at the neighbor's house at the very top of the hill, that I would focus on and walk towards that light. Anytime I took my focus off of that light and began wondering if anything was in the dark that might get me, I would turn my flashlight back on. I did this a few times until I was able to walk all the way up the hill in total darkness, only focusing on that light.

Proverbs 4:19

The way of the wicked is like darkness; they do not know over what they stumble.

I look at it this way now, God was preparing me to not fear the darkness inside of me so I could look at it and let it go. I put trust in that light to guide me to the top of the hill. Now I put my trust and faith in Jesus Christ. He lights my path for me.

Isaiah 42:16

"I will lead the blind by a way they do not know, in paths they do not know I will guide them. I will make darkness into light before them and rugged places into plains. These are the things I will do; and I will not leave them undone."

We are to always follow God's light, Jesus, no matter how dark the world seems to get around us. Following Jesus keeps us on the right path.

Sometimes we go through dark times and then there are times that are very bright, but no matter life's circumstances, always have faith and trust in God and keep your eyes on Jesus to get you through.

I had a fear of God, an unhealthy fear of God because I didn't understand God. I had a fear of letting God down. A fear that not doing the right things, because I wasn't. A fear of not being good enough for God to take me to Heaven. I was afraid of God's judgement. I was even afraid that God didn't actually exist. After listing this down, I realized that I had a fear of myself and my decisions because they always led to failure. My fear was that God was going to send me to hell. But after looking at it, my fear was of myself walking straight to hell because I was playing God in my life and other's lives by trying to control everything and everyone. I thought if I were able to control everything the way I thought things should be then life would be perfect and happy. All I did was make everyone mad at me or resentful towards me. No one likes to be controlled, not even me. Not by people anyway. I have to release control of my life to God every morning. Sometimes I don't do well at this step and take control back thinking I know what's best for me instead of waiting on God.

I had a fear of being alone/rejected. What I found when writing this out is that because of this fear, I closed myself off to others, thinking I was protecting myself from getting hurt. Well I actually became the rejector, rejecting others before they could reject me, which kept me alone and isolated. I did it to myself. The fear of being alone was much deeper than that. I was afraid to be alone with my thoughts. I was afraid that I would never be who "fill in the blank" wanted me to be. My thoughts lied to me. They told me that I never deserved this treatment or that treatment from others when I was the one causing the problems. My thoughts lied to me that I must have done something terribly wrong to be raped and beaten. My thoughts kept me in a very dark place and I didn't like it. I was afraid of me.

I had a fear of failure/success. This fear was because I never felt good enough for anything so when I would begin doing things well, and get promotions, I would self-sabotage which led to failure. I created it myself. I got to a point of, "why even try if I'm just going to fail".

I had a fear of living. I didn't know how to live. I was confused by society, religion, politics, self, everything. I didn't know who I was living for. I tried living for what everyone else wanted but I lost my identity doing this. I was afraid of not knowing who I was without validation from others. Living life by trying to please others leads to division of self and giving them power over your life.

I had a fear of death. Although I attempted suicide a few times, I was afraid to die. This fear, after looking at it led me to seeing that I was spiritually dead inside. I was afraid that there was absolutely nothing after death. I was a walking zombie, only surviving through life, not living it. I created this by feeding the sinful nature and not God's Holy Spirit.

I, at one time, had a fear of alcohol and drugs. I saw what drinking and using did to others and I didn't want to be that way. Holding tightly onto a fear, is what I became.

I had a fear of being lied to. Lies hurt people. Lies lead to no trust. Lies are exhausting and it's a vicious cycle of trying to keep up with what lie was told to whom. I was a liar.

Fear of being wrong. I never wanted to be wrong in anything, even if I was wrong. I wanted to always be right and always had to prove my side. I literally became the wrong in everything and even began accepting blame for every situation that every happened in my life. Much of it was my fought but I even accepted blame when others did something to me because it was easier to not argue.

Fear of abandonment. I'll make this one plain and simple. Afraid of being abandoned by God. So what did I do? I walked away from God when I was very young because I already felt abandoned by him.

I had a fear of Satan. I had seen so much evil in the world and I was terrified that Satan was going to take my soul from me. He was close to it that's for sure. Evil resided inside of me because of my actions, because of living a life full of sin instead of following the path led by Jesus.

I had many fears, but thought I would share these with you. I could see that everything I was afraid of, I created in my life. Everything begins and ends in the mind. We do not have to become our thoughts, we must become God's thoughts. Our thoughts are what separate us from God.

Then I got to the part of listing Harms to others. I'll just tell you that all of my harms to others came from my resentments list. How? Mostly due to retaliation, manipulation of my pain for my gain, unforgiving, controlling others, blaming, misunderstanding, self-seeking, selfish, lying, etc.

The sex harms list, well, let's just say I listed my marriages separately and lumped the others together. The harms were caused by me trying to build relationships from sex before even knowing if I liked the person or not. Then when I found out that I couldn't stand to be around them, I would leave. For the longest time, I had to drink to even have sex with anyone. Why? Because I didn't like it. Sex for me was mostly used as a means to get something, a means to have a place to stay, a means for self-confidence. Looking back, sex with only one person was actual love, the rest was just self-seeking. It wasn't intentional, just how I see it looking at life backwards.

After writing all of that out, I repented of all of it. My friend and I went through my life thoroughly. It was exhausting. When I finally had my hour with God, I took all of those papers and spread them out on the floor, giving all of that to God. Then a song popped into my head from when I was a child.

"Father, I adore you. I lay my life before you. How I love you".

"Jesus, I adore you, I lay my life before you. How I love you".

"Spirit, I adore you, I lay my life before you. How I love you".

This was the first time I truly cried over my past. This was the beginning of my healing. I begged God to forgive me for all of the horrible things that I did or even thought about doing. He did. But it took me quite awhile to begin forgiving myself.

I said that Kevin, my 2nd husband, would show up again in my story, he does. He found me on facebook and sent me a message. Remember, I had neither seen nor heard from him since 1994/95. His message to me was asking me, "what happened to us back then?". This stunned me because of how much time had passed. He still needed closure. He had no clue about the choices I had made in life after him or that I had just gotten out of a recovery center. I explained to him about my issues with alcohol back then, but didn't go into detail about me blaming him for anything. I took all blame on myself. He told me that I should have told him, he would have helped me. This conversation broke my heart because he was a really good guy. He had remarried and was doing well, he just needed closure. I apologized the best I knew how. He will show up again in my story because I didn't get everything out that I needed to and there was a reason why I needed to, I just didn't know why at this time. My thinking was that if I told him about all the things I blamed him for, in my mind, that would cause harm to him, so I didn't bring any of that up.

Awakening To Discernment Between God's Voice And Satan's Voice

After examining my life and repenting of all of my sins, some strange things began happening, but I didn't link them to the steps until much later. I was still in Florence in my apartment with Matt in his own room, me in my room and the other guy in the other room. My friend that I hated to ask to move out a couple of months prior asked for my help and I allowed her to come back to stay with us. I shared my room with her. One night after we all went to bed, my friend was asleep on an air mattress in my room and I was in my bed. I bolted up from a deep sleep because I thought I heard three loud knocks on my bedroom door. I was sitting up, wide awake at this point, a little scared when I heard a voice very loudly telling me not to open that door. It took me a little while to fall asleep after that because the voice scared me. I didn't open the door. The next morning, I asked Matt if he had knocked on my bedroom door the night before, he said that he hadn't and neither had our other roommate. Matt and I were not really talking much because I was not sure if I was supposed to be in a relationship with him or not. He was depressed all the time and isolated a lot. He was like that from the day he came to live with me in Florence. I tried my best to get him to do an evaluation of his life, but he insisted that didn't work for him and neither did the meetings, but he wasn't doing anything to get better. He went to counseling, but didn't like what they told him, so he didn't go back. He didn't want to hear things that would help him, he only wanted to continue thinking that no one understood him and he played the victim very well, just as I had all of my life before recovery. To be honest, nothing will work unless one is willing to work a program of recovery, whatever program one chooses.

Back to the strange things happening. I tried to figure out the meaning behind the knocking on the door and the voice telling me not to open it. I could come up with many meanings and still not quite sure what it meant. Looking back on it, I honestly believe it was Jesus knocking on the door and Satan telling me not to open it. I only believe this because of later events. Not only did I begin hearing voices, which I had trouble distinguishing between God and Satan, I began seeing a dark figure in my room at night. I used to refer to it as a shadow, but there was no light in the room for the shadow to form. Wow! After I typed that I finally put the last piece together. It would be a year later, that I realized what the dark figure was. I had just emptied all the darkness out of me. I knew that had been my darkness, very near, wanting to get back in. Now I know why I used to call it a shadow. The shadow formed was mine and it was able to form from the light within me, God's light was bright within me. The figure scared me for awhile. I thought it was going to harm me, but I began to ignore it. It was just there, not doing anything, just hanging around. I heard voices on and off and even told my brother, Richard, that I thought I was going insane. In the beginning, I honestly thought it was a warning to stay away from Matt and I got to a point that I thought Matt was going to kill me. That's how insane my mind went with this fear. Interestingly, the knocks on the door didn't scare me, just woke me up, only the voice scared me. That's how I discerned that the voice was not God. He does not create unhealthy fear in us.

Before I go on to the next events in my life, I want to share what I saw in my evaluation of my life, other than what I shared with you already. I was selfish, self-seeking, controlling, manipulating, full of rage, arrogant, blaming, unforgiving, and much more. There is no love in any of those behaviors, none. I didn't have a clue what love was. When my children would want to talk to me about school or things they did that they were proud of or things that upset them, I never wanted to hear any of it. I always brushed them off. I didn't care about what they wanted. They were my kids and they needed to want what I wanted. That's sick thinking right there. I didn't give my children the time of day. I left them to figure things out for themselves. How could I help them? My mind was so full of chaos,

I couldn't begin to put much more in it. The only things that come from a chaotic mind is chaos into the external world, outside of my being. I didn't know how to deal with myself, much less, anyone else's problems or them wanting attention. My entire problem was that I hated myself so much that I couldn't stand being with myself, ever. Because of that, I couldn't stand for anyone else to be around me either, unless I thought there was something in it for me, attention, love, alcohol, drugs, whatever it was, I was just selfish. No one can receive love or give love if they don't have it for themselves.

At the very end of February of 2019, my friend, Keri, received some devastating news. I should have been there to comfort her through this time of her life, but I wasn't. I had just moved back home with my parents because I couldn't stand being around Matt anymore. The negativity that he poured out was very draining to me. I told him that he could have the apartment as long as he paid the rent. As soon as I unloaded my things and put them in my room at my parents, I felt the need to face a fear that I had been holding onto for 8 months now. This was March 2, 2019, and instead of doing the next right thing, by being a good friend to Keri, I went to face Reign. I did what I wanted to do. I wasn't fully trusting God at this point because I still had fear of that situation. I knew he was going to kill me the last night I was there, I felt it. I knew that he had heard that I had talked about some things from that night. I had to find out for myself if he was looking for me to finish what he began or if it were all in my head. I know this was crazy and I know that I put myself in danger, but it was something that I felt I needed to do. I don't recommend anyone that is in recovery do what I did. Remember that I said while in the recovery center that I didn't tell myself that I could go without drugs for the rest of my life? Well, this is why. I knew that if I were going to face Reign, I would need to take a peace offering, a bag of meth. I knew that I would have to use with him when taking that peace offering over there. I talked to God about what I was going to do. I prayed about it. I even told God that I knew I would never touch a drug again after that day, and I haven't. I don't even think about wanting to use drugs. Anyway, I contacted someone that I knew that sold meth. I went and purchased a small bag, then went to see

Reign. I wasn't even scared when I got there. This was the house where everything happened that sent me to recovery for safety. When I knocked on his door, someone else answered. I knew him. He was pretty cool. He asked me what I was doing there. I told him that I came to see Reign. He said that Reign was sleeping. This guy tried many different ways to get me to leave, but I wasn't leaving until I was face to face with Reign, facing my fear.

I stayed there awhile that day and Reign finally woke up. He came out of his room and asked me what I was doing there. I told him that I just wanted to see how he was doing. I offered the dope to him and we smoked together. We were in his living room and I'm not even sure when the other man came in and sat down across from me on the other couch. He had been at the house the night everything went down. I'll call him Thorn. He just had a blank stare on his face, like he was looking right through me. That was kind of eerie, so I tried to make small talk with him. Reign went to his room and brought a book out and handed it to me telling me that I needed to read it. It was a book about satanic worship. I looked at it a minute, didn't read it though. Reign asked me if I wanted to go play in the woods, that's what we used to do all the time, so I said "sure". He went to his laundry room and then was standing behind me as I was sitting on the couch. I looked back and saw that he was holding a sickle. I looked back at Thorn, then the book, and I said to Reign without turning around, "what are you going to do, chop my head off?". He replied, "no, this is for the brush". We never used anything to knock weeds down in the woods, we just trampled over them. It was silence for a moment and I acted like I was reading that book. So, I stood up, looked at Reign and said, "ok, I'm ready to go play in the woods now". His response was, "I don't want to anymore". Ya'll this dude was going to take me out and I wasn't even scared. Do you know why I wasn't scared? Because I had The almighty powerful God with me. I truly believe that Reign saw that too. Not long later Reign began talking to me about that last night I was there. He was rambling off names and said I needed to know them. I put my fingers in my ears like a child would and was saying, "lalalalalalalalalala, I don't want to hear it. It's none of my business". I didn't hear it either, because I didn't allow myself to. When I walked into his room, that's when I noticed all the writings on his bedroom door, especially the bold letters that said, "the evil one". As I walked into his room, a dark floating figure caught my eye. I even swatted at this thing. Reign said, "they're everywhere in here". Those were dark spirits. It was death. I felt it, yet I stayed longer. Before I left, Reign was telling me that he was afraid to leave his house to work because he didn't want anyone else stealing his stuff. Well, he's the one that allowed those people in his home. Before I walked out of his house, I told him that he was a fungus that was growing attached to his house because he couldn't separate himself from it. I felt a little bad about that, and even apologized. Before I left though, I did take him to get something to eat. He had nothing and probably had not eaten in days. Why would I do this? Because he's still a human being and needed food.

I went back to my parent's and began feeling very uneasy. I kept getting into my head that I had put myself and now my family in danger by going to see Reign. I allowed fear back in. So, I ran. That's what I did best. I found an oxford house in Charleston, SC and moved there within a week. It was beautiful there. I had trouble finding a job and my mom told me that if I didn't find a job by the end of the month, I would have to come back home because she wasn't going to pay over a month's rent for me. All of these things were tests that I failed miserably. Repeated behaviors. When the end of the month came, I still had no job. I packed my things into my car and was going to go home. I had spoken to Matt a few times during the time I was in Charleston. I contacted him the morning I was leaving Charleston to see if he was ok with me coming back to the apartment. I was on the interstate driving towards home when I saw the exit approaching that went to Florence. For the first time I could see the crossroads. Which one do I take? Do I go home feeling like a failure again or do I go to Florence with Matt? I didn't want to go home feeling like a failure again, I saw this exit and remembered what Matt had told me many times. "I'll do anything for you. I'll take care of you". So what did I do? I took that exit and headed to Florence. In my mind, it was still my apartment anyway. I knew he would take care of me, so that's where I went trying to convince myself that I loved him when I knew that his behavior only hurt me. This was April 2019. This is when I learned that you don't have to be open and honest about everything you've ever done. My honesty about things I had done while away from Florence for those couple of months only caused Matt to have no trust for me whatsoever. By admitting things to Matt, he couldn't let it go and always threw it in my face if we argued. I apologized countless times, but none of it mattered to Matt. So the last week of April, I decided I truly couldn't deal with this and decided to move back home, failures and all. When Matt found out this was my plan, a friend told him while he was at work, Matt came home at lunch that day and said he had been fired due to something that happened the week prior. I'm sorry, but I don't know of any company that will allow you to work a half of a day, knowing they're going to fire you due to errors one made the week prior. I could be wrong on that, but that's how I felt. I felt like he quit his job because he knew I was leaving again. I felt so bad because I was responsible for him leaving Greenville to move to Florence. I felt totally responsible for him. So after a week of staying in Florence with him, I moved him with me to my parents. Although I was in recovery and free from drugs and alcohol, except that one day, I was still acting on the insanity of my thoughts. While living with my parents, I still saw that shadow and at this point, I thought it was following Matt.

We began attending church at Newspring in Columbia, SC. I felt more welcome there than I did in the one in Florence. I think it was just me though. I had grown some, but not much. I was seeking truth about God and myself and about what love truly meant. Matt and I decided to go to the connect groups because we wanted to serve in church. I wanted to start giving back by serving. After completing these classes, I wanted to sign up to teach the connect classes, but while in line, God nudged me over to sign up for Kidspring. I signed up to serve with Kidspring and had to go through an interview first. I was on fire for Jesus and talked a lot about recovery with Sharon, the lady that interviewed me. I talked a lot because I was so excited about being able to give back. I was open and honest with her about my past. The next Sunday, I went to a "first look" at Kidspring. There were a few of us in the room learning about the different areas of Kidspring, the rules, etc. Remember I said that while in the recovery center that I had stated I was supposed to work with special needs children? Well, it came to me right in that room that Sunday. One of the classes was for special needs children and as soon as I heard about that classroom, I knew that's where God wanted me to be. It was a year prior that I had announced that out loud in the meeting in recovery. The following Sunday was my first time serving in this classroom and I loved it. I wasn't sure why God put me there, but I was there. I probably drove my teammates nuts with incessantly talking about things I had learned in recovery and on and on about myself and addictions. They were very patient with me and I'm grateful for that! It was the second week serving that I found out what God was teaching me. One of the older kids, autistic, had a routine of playing the basketball game, telling you his score and a fist bump, then he would go to the clock and say the time out loud and start all over again. After about his third time in this routine, I had gotten up from my seat and noticed that no one fist bumped this kid and after he said the time out loud, I interrupted his pattern and asked him his score and gave him a fist bump. He looked at me very weird and stood there a moment. I had noticed as well, that when the younger kid's patterns were disrupted, they would become chaotic and we would have to redirect them to something different or back to their pattern. Then he started his routine over again. What I learned from this is that we all have patterns in life that we tend to follow. Some good, some bad. Early in life, I actually wanted to follow Jesus, although I didn't understand him, but I didn't follow Jesus because I wanted to fit in with others and didn't want to be ridiculed for being a "Jesus freak". Along my path in life, each and every temptation that I fell into caused chaos and separation from the right path. God wanted me to walk the straight and narrow path and avoid temptations, just as Jesus showed us how to do in the bible. I allowed every temptation to keep me off of the straight and narrow and lived in a world of chaos. I became addicted to the chaos after living in it for so long. When I got sober, it was difficult to be still and at peace because I didn't know how to live without the chaos. That kid taught me that just because a disruption comes along your path, and they will, I don't have to panic. I only have to walk through the chaos to get to the other side. It only took him a few seconds to get right back into his pattern that kept him calm. When I feel like I'm being tempted, I turn right back to God to keep me away from the chaos and in God's peace.

Matt wanted to serve on the prayer team, but he was told that they didn't think he was ready for that yet. I can tell you he wasn't happy about it and thought that they just didn't like him. He served as a greeter.

We were in church one Sunday, or I was, and I heard the story of the Samaritan woman at the well. I had heard this story before, quite a few times, but I listened to it this time. When I heard the story, Matt and I were not yet married. The part that astonished me was John 4:16-18 "Go and get your husband," Jesus told her. "I don't have a husband," the woman replied. Jesus said, "you're right! You don't have a husband-for you have had five and you aren't even married to the man you're living with now. You certainly spoke the truth!".

After reading this, I began feeling guilty. I had five ex-husbands and the man I was living with, well, we weren't married. This was my story. So, on June 19, 2019, Matt and I got married. I thought this is what God was telling me to do. I was trying my best to understand God, but I still didn't understand God. We both married, knowing inside of us that neither of us wanted to marry but neither of us admitted it at the time. The only motive I had, that I can think of was, if we're going to get married anyway, why not get married now and I could be put on his insurance at work. Also, I married him out of guilt for living in sin. We had planned to marry on his one year of recovery, but instead married three months earlier.

So, we're living at my parent's and I had not had a job since October of 2018. This was now June of 2019. It wasn't for lack of trying, I promise you that. I applied for so many jobs online. I received rejection letter after rejection letter. I didn't allow that to keep me down though. My mom kept telling me that I needed to apply for this or apply for that. I had to tell her, I've already applied for those positions. I reminded her that I trusted God and was being patient because I knew God would bring me a job. Not long after this, one Sunday morning before Kidspring classes began, I was there early talking with a wonderful friend, Alli, in our little classroom. She asked me how my job search was going. I told her that it wasn't. I kid you not, right then and there, she received a text message from a lady in church that was looking for someone to help with her company. Alli said, "look, there's God right there", pointing to her phone. She asked me if she could give this lady my name and number, "of course" was my reply. The only thing I knew about the job was that it was at a gymnastics center and I knew nothing about gymnastics, but God put it there. I figured it wouldn't hurt to check it out anyway.

God Spoke To Me Today!
And I obeyed.

The next day, Monday, I picked Matt up from work as usual. He worked third shift so I picked him up that morning. We had not been doing well but stayed together. It was convenient. We were arguing this day and he went to the bedroom and I was sitting at the table. I don't remember what I was thinking, but that's when I heard God loud and clear for the first time ever! I had been talking to God out loud for about a month, questioning everything and being grateful for everything. How did I know it was God's voice? Well, it surely wasn't mine. I know my voice well. It was as if this thought, or voice consumed my entire being. As soon as I heard it, I looked up, tears streaming down my face and said, "I'm not doing that". I argued with God because I didn't want to do what he was asking of me. The voice didn't go away. It was more like a very loud thought, the only thought in my head and it was a beginning to end thought of what God was telling me to do. I truly didn't want to do this. What was God asking? He wanted me to pray. Pray out loud, with Matt, over our relationship. So, I mustered up some courage and walked in the bedroom and asked Matt if I could pray for us. Tears were just streaming down my face. It was difficult because I had just said some very ugly words to Matt during our argument. It took a few minutes for any words to come out of my mouth, but I did it. I think this was the hardest thing that I had ever done in my life. I don't remember the words, and it wasn't the words that mattered. It was that I finally heard God and I obeyed. The very next morning, which was a Tuesday, after picking Matt up from work, there God was again, full thought of what he wanted me to do, and there were the tears again. We arrived home and Matt went to bed. I sat outside on the back step smoking a cigarette and talking to God. I said, "ok, God, I know what you want me to do, but when?". It was something God wanted me to tell my dad. It was simple really, but difficult too. So, "God, I know my dad is at work. Should I wait for him to get home or go see him at work?". I'm waiting for an answer from God and my mom calls me. She said, "Paige, I need you to make your daddy lunch and take it to him at work. I have a dr.'s appointment". After we hung up the phone, I said, "ok, God, I hear you loud and clear". So I had the what, the where. The why and the how didn't matter, I knew I needed to obey God. I did what I was told to do. My brother, Rusty, heard me talking to daddy while at the office. Rusty called me into his office and said, "that's tough isn't it, when God pulls on your heartstrings?". Anyway, Rusty asked me if I wanted to fill in at the family business temporarily because one of their workers was out from surgery. I accepted because I hadn't had a job in a while and my intentions were now good. I wasn't out to take anyone's position from them. I was grateful that my brother asked me to fill in. I was just grateful. Then on Wednesday, I received a phone call from a lady that worked for the gymnastics place that Alli had given my name and number to. She asked if I would be interested in doing an interview the next day. I said that I would be there and she gave me the address.

I called Rusty and told him that I wouldn't be able to fill in with the family company because although I was only going for an interview, I already knew that I had the job. I don't know how I knew, I just did and I didn't even know what the job consisted of. Thursday I went to the interview, not knowing how to dress because I wasn't exactly sure what I was interviewing for. Well, I found out that it was for after-school care with 60-65 children between the ages of 4-12. My first thought was heck no. hahahaha My second thought was, "shut up Paige, God just gave you a job that you didn't even apply for". So I accepted the job. After that was finalized and I was filling out paperwork as an employee, one of the owners and I were talking. This is the lady that had texted Alli on Sunday morning. My new boss, said, I would have called you sooner, but one of our current employees had offered to fill that position, but on Monday, her college schedule changed. I then had to tell my "new" boss what happened on Monday. The first time I heard God and obeyed what he told me to do. God worked all of this out. So, again, me and my thinking thought this must be for some great purpose God has for me. I went into this job thinking that there were things that maybe needed improvement, etc. What arrogance I had. Nope, I found out that God's purpose, so far, has been about my growth with him. I learned a lot of patience working with these children. I loved this position. God also taught me through these children that I am loveable.

Matt had a good job, I had just begun working and seemed like maybe life would get better for the two of us. Something was missing though, neither of us were going to meetings, which he didn't like going to anyway. The most important thing missing was God leading our marriage.

We had just moved out of my parent's into a one bedroom house a few blocks from my parent's. I stayed there at nights by myself while he worked and he was there in the day by himself while I worked. Matt wouldn't talk to me about his feelings, what he was thinking, what he wanted to do, nothing. I would get so irritated and frustrated that it came out in anger. Matt isolated, even when I was home. It's difficult trying to be in a relationship when one or both of you are closed off completely. Instead of him telling me how he felt about things, he would try and point blame at me for doing things I wasn't doing. He wouldn't talk with me, he wouldn't interact with me, but he wanted sex. I didn't want anything to do with the sex because of him being so closed off to me. I wanted the emotional connection before the physical connection. He only wanted the physical aspect of a relationship. We were not of the same mind, the mind of God was not with us.

He and I did a lot of work on this little house but it still needed more work. It was livable, just unfinished. I will say that he did keep the house clean while I was at work. We didn't get along well at all. I tried. One day, I was cleaning the back room that had a lot of tools and supplies in it and I found a half empty beer can. A 22oz beer can. I was not happy. We were both supposed to be staying clean and sober together. I asked him about it. He told me that he meant to throw it away, but forgot. He said he and the neighbor were sitting on the porch one day before I got home from work and it was the neighbor's beer. I believed everything except it being the neighbor's beer. Why wouldn't the neighbor just take it back to his house instead of Matt trying to hide it behind a board in the back room? I didn't argue about it though. I already had suspicions of him drinking and using anyway because of a few things he had told me. I will tell you this, God used Matt in a mighty way to begin to change me though. Matt would fuss at me about being on facebook. My response? "Well, you're on it too". Those types of responses only cause arguments. I would ask Matt about him chatting with women, he would get mad and tell me that I was the one chatting with men. I wasn't. I never kept my phone locked, but he did. I even offered to let him go through my phone anytime he wanted to, he always refused. After taking him to work at night, I began talking to God a lot. "God, why do I have to stop using facebook if he isn't? Why do I have to change if he isn't?" Do you know what God told me? His reply, "because I said so. Because I'm making an example out of you". This is when I began seeing total truth about myself and my reactions. It hurt my ego badly, but I began to pause before reacting. I began doing things differently. I would cry a lot during this time because looking at my actions as they were happening and being able to see them, and then finally being able to pause before acting on them was huge. Painful, but huge for me. I was finally putting things I learned into practice, humbling myself before God, giving God my anger or pain, and reacting differently than I always had.

One night, after taking him to work, I was almost back home when a car got behind me and followed me to the house. This scared me. It was about 10:30 or 11:00 at night. I got out of my car and the guy had stopped in the road with his window rolled down. I asked him if I could help him. I knew he was a dealer, but didn't let on that I knew that. He asked me where the guy was that lived here. I asked him, "what guy"? He got nervous and was pointing in all directions and I looked at him and said, "I just moved here, I'm not sure who you're talking about". I knew exactly who he was talking about, he was referring to the man I just married. I only know this because of a story Matt told me about a guy he ran into by the river that tried to sell him cocaine. We tell on ourselves when we don't even realize it. This realization didn't occur to me until later though. One night when I came home from work, I didn't get home until around 7pm, Matt was literally passed out in the bed. He denied everything I asked him about, so again, I didn't argue. We agreed to go to counseling. I made an ass out of myself because Matt wouldn't talk about anything and I had gotten so frustrated with our entire marriage, that I looked like the entire problem. The last argument we got into, I was irritated because he was asleep when I got home from work when he could have slept all day. I was irritated because he wanted sex but refused to even have conversations with me. I was irritated because he would say he wanted to go out and do things, but when we went to Columbia, he wouldn't tell me what he wanted to do. He left those decisions to me and if it wasn't the right decision, he would blame me for never doing anything he wanted to do. I was irritated because I knew that he was chatting with other women. I was irritated because he was watching porn movies while I was at work. I had been holding these feelings in for a short while and I let them out with me yelling at him to please just talk to me. He yelled, called me all kinds of names, accused me of all kinds of things that I wasn't doing, cursed and for the first time ever, I just sat there and let him vent with no reaction from me. I looked at him and said, "I'm going to my parent's. When you calm down and feel like talking, I'll come back". Matt's response to me was, "if you leave, don't come back. Leave your ring and take your things". He walked out the front door and slammed it. I just sat there. I realized for the first time in a long time, I had a choice. It's my choice. I could stay and continue this chaos between the two of us or I could leave. I packed my things, took my ring off, laid it on the table and left. This was a little taste of freedom for me for the first time ever. Not the freedom you may be thinking of, but freedom to make my own decision and be ok with it. Not long later, I was talking with someone from church and they told me that "God doesn't like divorce". This stung and reminded me that I already had 5 failed marriages behind me and this would be number 6. Guilt started to creep in. I talked to God a lot about this. My guilt, failure, all of it, and I went back to Matt for about a week and a half. My guilt drove me there. When I left the last time, I was calm. I told him how sorry I was. I told him that it was never my intentions to hurt him. I told him that I had never wanted to be in a relationship, with anyone, from the beginning. He even admitted to me that he had not wanted to get married. I left on friendly terms. I even offered to continue taking him to work if he needed a ride, and I did a few times. It took me a couple of times to break the connection between he and I . Do you know why? Because anytime you are intimate with someone, you're connecting your souls. It is so much more than just sex. It's deeper than that. So if you meet someone and have sex before getting to know them and then when you actually get to know them, and you don't like each other, it's still hard to disconnect because of the soul connection. That's why it's extremely important to date first. Get to know each other first. Be friends. No holding hands or kissing until you get to a point of knowing whether you even like each other as individuals, not just in bed. God created sex and gave it to us as a very fragile but powerful gift. When we mistreat that gift, the power of it controls us to stay in unhealthy relationships that should have never been.

After I finally broke free, I still had a little guilt and shame and I blamed myself for all of it for awhile. I know better now. We both played a role in it.

I kept seeing that scripture pop up at church and in devotionals about the Samaritan woman. I told God, "I left him, what are you trying to tell me?". It wasn't but about a week or two later that I found out that Matt was still legally married to his first wife. That's what God was telling me, it wasn't a legal marriage. The guilt was gone and we were both free. Well, it took almost a year later for me to get the annulment approved, but it was. I cannot say anything else about Matt, because after I left, his business was no longer mine. I can only pray for him to find God.

In November 2019, I was at work one day and one of the little girls told me that I smelt like smoke. One girl said she liked the smell because one of her relatives smoked, the other little girl said that she didn't like it. I went home that day and decided to quit smoking, and I did. The second week I noticed that I was eating a lot more. I had to push back from the food a little, not all of it. I liked my snacks, don't judge. Then I began doing something that I never liked doing before, shopping for shoes and clothes. One day I was in Belk's with my arms full of clothes. I looked down at them and put them all back and left. I realized what was going on. I had replaced cigarettes with food, then food with shopping. It's a vicious cycle of addictions. Everything was going pretty good. I can't think of anything major that happened between November 2019 and January 2020.

January 2020, I met a man at one of my meetings. I thought he "was the one". I couldn't get this man out of my head. He even went to the same church that I did. During one of my women's bible study groups one of the ladies told me she knew someone perfect for me. Yep, the guy that I was "addicted" to. She had no clue. This led me to believe that God was talking through her and he really was the one. I'm not sure how long passed but one Sunday afternoon, I couldn't get those thoughts out of my head. No meeting was going on at this time, so I decided to go back to church for the 5 pm service. It was the same as the morning service. I had to look at my thoughts though. I had different underlying motives. I was hoping to see this guy at church. My mind was insane and I couldn't get it to stop. After church, I was driving home on the interstate just talking to God like I always did and I happened to look up to my right…..a huge billboard that I had never noticed before…….LUST DESTROYS, JESUS SAVES. I laughed out loud and said, "God you've got jokes, but I hear you".

I don't remember exactly when this was, but sometime early in 2020, I was on facebook just scrolling through and that legend appeared of "people you may know" and the first picture I saw was of the guy that beat me black and blue and tried to rape me 20 years prior. My first thought was why am I seeing him? Then I knew why. This is when I found out how to do a true amends with something from my past. I sent him a private message apologizing for my part in that mess that night that he and I were all over each other and he ended up beating me from head to toe. I never brought up anything he did to me, I only apologized for flirting all night long with him, then lying to everyone else about it. He responded immediately and I wasn't sure what his reaction would be. He said, "never in a million years did I expect to hear from you". He then thanked me and told me how much that helped him. He said, "you're an angel sent from God". I wasn't expecting it, but he also said that he was sorry for the things he did to me that night and said that wasn't him that night. I told him that I had already forgiven him for that but thanked him anyway. Do you know what I learned from this? If I want God to forgive me of my wrongs and free me of my guilt and shame, I should do the same for others. I can help set them free of some of their guilt. It would be totally selfish of me to only want forgiveness for myself and continue holding a resentment towards someone else. These small things are very freeing and healing, not just for self, but others as well. Jesus says to love others as he loves us. This begins to bring people together as one and takes away the division between us all. When we have arguments with each other, someone does something bad to us or we do something bad to them, until the situation is addressed, there is always division. The division is there because one is holding onto guilt and the other is holding onto a resentment. It's time we begin healing and taking away that division. If you're the one holding onto a resentment and waiting for the other to apologize, you may be waiting a long time. Sometimes people get over things and forget about them, not even realizing you're mad at them. Sometimes you must forgive without an apology. If you're the one that caused a harm to someone, no matter how long ago it was, be the bigger person and make a step towards amending these situations with each other. We need to bring love back into our lives. We can't just sit around waiting for everyone else to come to us to fix situations, we have to be bold and step into that boldness and take action.

March 2020, Covid hits. The company I worked for closed and we were all out of work. Many people were out of work, school, church, everything closing down.

The end of March, early April a guy contacted me through messenger about wanting help with recovery. I was leery of this because I didn't know if he actually wanted help or if he was trying to play me. I was beginning to think better and make better decisions. So I called my buddy, Allen, who was in Kentucky working as an interventionalist. I need to flashback a minute. I went to one of my meetings in Columbia about a month prior to this and Allen was there, at my homegroup meeting. I had to explain to him who I was and where we knew each other from. Anyway, he told me that he was on his way back to Kentucky and he gave me his business card. I didn't even know that he was in Kentucky or that he had his own business until I saw him.

Back to the situation with this guy texting me on facebook. He lived in Spokane, WA and I had not clue how to help him. I called Allen and told him about the situation and gave him the guys name and number. Allen called me back and said that the guy was serious about getting help. I knew this guy didn't have any money so I told Allen I would get him a bus ticket to Kentucky if he could find a recovery center for him. We had it planned out and I purchased the ticket for the guy to be in Kentucky in a few days. The next day I thought, hey, I'm not working right now, I could go to Kentucky and meet this guy when he gets off of the bus. So I called Allen and asked him about that. He said, yeah, come on up. He gave me the address and I packed my things and headed to Kentucky. The only thing I didn't consider was everything being closed due to covid. Thank goodness it was only a 5 hour trip and gas stations were open. It was a great trip too. Not much traffic at all, no one traveling due to covid. It was beautiful in the mountains, very peaceful. I had my radio blaring to K-love and I was singing and praising God all the way to Kentucky. It was good seeing Allen and meeting his friends. I considered this a very spiritual journey and I learned discernment the couple of days I was there.

Not everything went as planned. The guy in Spokane called me while I was at Allen's and told me he couldn't get a ride to the bus station and needed someone to pay for his uber. I got on the phone with the driver and gave him my card info, we were on video chat so, I felt safter about that. Then other things happened and the guy missed a bus transfer due to being sick from withdrawal and was left in the cold. We googled the temperature where the guy was and it was freezing and snowing if I remember correctly. So I talked with a hotel and got him a room for the night. The next morning, one of Allen's friends, asked me if I was willing to spend all of my money, if needed, to get this guy to Kentucky. I told her that I would do that, as long as I had money to get back home. She then said, God will reward you for this. We didn't hear from the guy for awhile and I was getting worried that he wouldn't make it. He asked me if I'd send him a little money to get just a beer to help him get through the sickness of withdrawals so he could get back on the bus. I was willing to do this. After talking with him on the phone, he was serious. All I had to do was get him a little money for food and beer. So, we didn't do everything right, I didn't send the money. I still think if I had sent the money, he would have made it to Kentucky. Instead, he got a return trip to Spokane, WA. He apologized to me and told me that he just got really scared because of the withdrawals from not only alcohol but heroin as well. I learned a lot from this experience. I truly wish I had done more for him because I know he wanted help.

I was planning on staying one more day in Kentucky, but for some reason after lunch, I felt the need to leave so I could make it to a meeting in Columbia, SC. I left right around 3 and the meeting started at 8pm. I made it about 20 minutes late. I was trying to share my experience but I was tired. I know they all misunderstood what I was trying to share, but it didn't matter. I made it back. After the meeting, I was walking to my car and one of the men called my name as he was walking towards me. He handed me a lighthouse coin. I couldn't see it because it was dark, but it was a little heavier than a normal chip. I thanked him and went home. When I got home to look at it, I realized this was my reward from God for trying my best to help that guy get to a treatment facility. On the front of the coin is a lighthouse, on the back it says, "God let your light shine through me like a fog light so those who are lost, sick and dying find your love through me. Amen". I cried when I read that because I knew that was my reward from God for my efforts and never getting angry or resentful when the guy turned around because he got scared. I understood. I also, received another coin later that says on the front: Love, Honesty, Unselfishness, Purity. Those are gifts from God that he gave me. That's how I try and live my life everyday.

May 2020. I had been visiting a friend of mine at a sober living house in Columbia and we began hanging out and building a good friendship. I was still living at home with my parents and wanted to move to Columbia but couldn't afford it because I had only been working about 25-30 hours a week. Besides, I was still out of work due to covid. The end of May came around and I was contacted by the owner of the company, well, we all were, to let us know about a meeting at work to discuss the changes before going back to work.

So I went to this meeting and my boss states that all after-school workers won't start until the first week of June, but Paige, you will start Monday. She then asked me to see her in her office after the meeting. I felt like I was in trouble. So my position was changed to working in the front reception area. I know why, although she didn't tell me. I still had some growing to do. Besides, I did well with office work, that's mostly all I've done most of my life. I loved it up front. I can remember a few times being frustrated as I was learning to do things up front. I knew I couldn't handle them the way I used to. My old self would have thrown a fit and yelled and probably walked out the front door and never gone back. God was definitely teaching me how to live differently. Well, it began when I was with Matt, but it never stops. Learning in a work environment is different because you're around the public and I didn't want to show anyone how I used to act.

One day when I became very frustrated, I knew everyone could see the frustration on my face, I got up from the desk and went to the bathroom. I got on my knees and prayed. I asked God to help me through this. Honestly what I was getting so upset about wasn't anything that major, just my mind wanted to make it into something major. I was beginning to see before acting and beginning to create new reactions; reacting with kindness, love and humility. That was hard! Praying to God helped tremendously. I was able to let it go much quicker than I had in the past. I wasn't sitting there stewing on something in my head trying to justify where I was right. I just let it go.

Not long after going back to work, my boss asked me if I was still interested in cleaning the gym on the weekends. Of course, I was. I had been talking with my mom about wanting to move to Columbia to be closer to my meetings, church, and work. I told her that I was given the opportunity to clean the gym on the weekends, so I could most likely afford to live in the sober living home where my friend was. The next morning, I went to visit my friends at sober living and was talking with a new girl, she asked me to sponsor her. We had a great walk and talk at the Riverwalk. On my way home, I was talking to God and asking if I was doing a good job and leading this girl in the right direction. My phone rang in the middle of my conversation with God. It was my mom. She told me that if I thought I was ready to move out and I thought that the sober living house was a good fit, she would forgo my car payment for that month and that would help me with the move in deposit. This was a confirmation to me from God that I was doing the right things and he was rewarding me for it. When I looked at how much I was being paid to clean the gym and how much weekly rent was, I was dumbfounded. God always provides! Always! Never doubt that. The amount of pay for the weekend work was five dollars more than the weekly rent at sober living. So, I moved into the Oxford House that weekend.

This was a test for me. I never really got along with females and now I was moving into a house full of them. We all got along for the most part. There were times that I became very frustrated or angry about something, but I handled those things much better than I would have in the past. It was small things that I got angry over too. When I looked at why I was angry, it wasn't because of someone doing something wrong to me, it was because someone would point out where I was wrong. My ego didn't like that. I had much more growing to do. I had to look to see where they were right in what they were saying and I had to change things that I was doing wrong. God used all of these women to help shape me into a better person, but I had to be willing to listen and accept what they were saying before I could actually change and grow.

September 2020

My good friend, Lashawn, was contacted by a recovery home, that she once worked at briefly, asking if she were ready to come back to work there. She and I talked about it and I told her that she should go. It would be great experience for her. The next day she came to me and said that she wasn't going to go, that she had recommended someone else for the position. Then she told me that she had recommended me. Well, I was not expecting that. I had a good job that I loved. I had a great church family. I had a great AA homegroup. I told her that I would have to pray about that, and I did. That following Sunday as I was sitting in church and was listening to the message. It was the story of Moses and the burning bush. The 'angel of the Lord' appeared in the burning bush and was speaking to Moses. Moses was thanking God for coming to help his people. God said, "no, I'm sending you". I literally sat back in my chair and said, "God, is this for me?". Then the pastor circled those two words on the screen, "sending you". I said, "I hear you God". But I still wasn't fully convinced. After church, I went home to the Oxford House and I saw something sitting on the floor outside of my bedroom door. As I got closer, I saw it. It was a ceramic angel that one of my roommates placed there for me. She had no clue what I was praying about. I took that as a sign of the 'Angel of the Lord' appearing to me, leading me into where he wanted to send me. So, after I changed clothes, I went to the gym to clean. I had my music blaring as I always did when I cleaned the gym. I remembered what my boss asked of me not too long ago. When you leave, please give me at least a month's notice. Well, I didn't have a month's notice to give her, it would be 3 weeks at best. I had not even talked with the people that owned the recovery home before calling my boss and giving her that 3 week's notice. I already knew this is where God was sending me. I knew nothing about what my duties would be or the pay, it didn't matter, I was following where God was sending me. Then I called the owner of the recovery home and set up an interview for that Tuesday. They hired me. I went there for the first two weekends and stayed there to get a feel for what I would be doing. The very first weekend, I went to church with them. The pastor got on the stage and was telling us that he had a great message prepared for today, but God woke him up early that morning and told him that he had to give another message for someone special this morning. He had no clue what was going on in my head, but God did. I don't remember that sermon either, I only remember two words from it, "I'm here". Yes, I was here. The third weekend I moved from Columbia, to Graniteville, SC to work as a manager of this recovery home. I had no clue what I was getting myself into. After a few weeks, I felt like I had been thrown into a lion's den. I had been in recovery for just over two years, with one and a half years of continuous sobriety. At one point, I worked here by myself, seven days a week, waking up at 3:30 am and working until 10pm. I didn't get any days off, but we got through those days together. I cried a lot during the first couple of months. It was very difficult not knowing exactly what to do, how to handle situations that arose, how to be firm and loving, how to stop being afraid of confrontation, how to learn to stop being a people pleaser, and learn how to be true to myself and my position as manager. I didn't do things perfectly. I failed at many things, but I learned through those failures. I knew this was a temporary position when I went there, that was God's promise to me, not because the owner's wanted me temporarily. Again, this was another job I walked into thinking I was sent there for a my great purpose and I wanted to change things. Some things did need changing, but I had a difficult time following through with the change because most times, change is met with resistance. I allowed resistance to keep me just doing what I was already doing. I had a very difficult time separating myself as staff from being a friend to the women living in the home. I had a difficult time separating my recovery from theirs. It felt more like a family. The problem with that is when you're like a family, the ones in the program will learn your weaknesses and know how to manipulate your weakness to get their way. That's what we as addicts do, manipulate and control others to have things our way. I may not have been as strong as I wanted to be when leaving this position, but I came out a much stronger person than when I went in. I have to remind myself all the time that the greater purpose is never for me to understand and mostly about God teaching me something and building me up for something better. I saw many things about myself that I needed to see and begin to let go of and have more faith while walking into God's next purpose for my life.

To this day, the only purpose that I can see is God teaching me and molding me. How he uses me, I have no clue, but I know he does. He uses all of us when we stop playing God and just be loving in everything that we do.

Obedience

Proverbs 10:17 (NLT)

People who accept discipline are on the pathway to life, but those who ignore correction go astray.

Another version of this same verse:

Whoever heeds discipline shows the way to life, but whoever ignores correction leads others astray. (dailyverses.net)

When I first began obeying God, I honestly didn't like it. It was extremely painful. Becoming obedient to God, meant that I had to stop doing things the same way that I did them throughout life. It is not easy changing your ways, but it is very possible. You become a totally new person. Basically, what you do is kill the old self by making your sinful nature bow down before God. (Which is what I wanted to do for many years, kill myself, not realizing that it was ego that needed to die) To those that think that a drug can kill the ego, I'm sorry, but you're sadly mistaken. The only thing that will kill your ego is listening to what others say you are doing that hurts them and letting go of foolish pride.

One example of this is that I used to always react negatively when someone would point out my wrongs. My immediate reaction was to deny that I was doing those things and turn the blame around on them. Changing this took time and patience with myself. When I first began to see my own behaviors, it was always after I had just reacted badly. I would apologize immediately, but then fall right into the same behaviors that same day or the next day. I don't even remember how long this went on, but I can remember getting so frustrated with myself because I immediately saw how I was in the wrong after I acted on the old behavior and would apologize, then beat myself up for it. I couldn't understand why I was still doing the same things over and over again. Trust me when I say it wasn't easy. My ego was bruised badly almost constantly. Then one day, I began to see my behavior as I was in it and when I could see it halfway through an angry rant, I was able to stop it. More practice and more practice, but progress! Then it happened! I was able to pause when agitated or doubtful. I was able to act on new, better behaviors than I had in the past. It hurt, because I wanted to do what I had always done. These changes did not come easily for me. I prayed a lot. I asked God to give me strength to let go of the old and the courage to create the new.

I used to think I was a good person. I was good when I wanted to be good. I was good at some really bad things as well. One day, years ago, I even made the statement out loud that if I couldn't be good, I would just be good at being bad, and those are behaviors I practiced. Bad ones. Over time, I became good with bad behaviors and I even bragged about them.

But I didn't like myself and did things that were against my true nature. It didn't matter how much I thought about being different or being a better person, thinking doesn't create the change, only taking the action to become different is where the change comes in. Before you are able to change anything about yourself, you must be willing to hear what someone is saying to you instead of deflecting it back on them. You have to see where others are right and where you may be wrong. You have to see the behavior before you can change it. Otherwise, you're still the same person, only thinking you're different. When you listen, no matter how painful, you will begin to see yourself and your actions as they come out of you.

It's like when you're growing up and your parents are teaching you to obey them. If you don't obey them, there are consequences for disobedience. The same goes for when you are born again. Now you are being corrected by your heavenly father and when you don't follow the correction there are consequences. Usually the consequences are constantly arguing with others because you can never see where you are wrong but you only see where others are wrong. This is total denial of self. Self-awareness is key. We can all see other's actions because they are in front of us. Seeing self takes so much more willingness and honesty. I began using people as my mirror. What I saw in others that I didn't like was a reflection of things I didn't like about myself. When I would see something that I didn't like in another person, I would begin to immediately ask myself, do I act like that? Do I do the things they're doing? Then I had to reflect on events in my life to look at my actions in circumstances, not other's actions. Remember, you cannot change anyone but yourself, no matter how hard you try. The only person you can control is yourself.

I began reading the bible more as well. Reading the bible convicted me on a lot of my behaviors and helped me change and grow.

I also listened in meetings to what others were saying and how they got through tough situations.

While learning how to change, I wasn't always correct in my thinking. My thinking was that I could just ask God to remove my sins, then I was changed. Boy, was I wrong. God showed me where I was wrong too, many times.

Anytime my feelings or ego was hurt, I would have to pause and think about the situation. Did someone truly do something to hurt me or was my ego just bruised? Or if someone did hurt my feelings, I had to pause, give God my first reaction and thoughts, which would have been anger, then responding in a different way than I ever did before in life, responding with grace and mercy. That takes much practice. What I learned through practicing this step is that people are just people and no one makes me mad or angry, I allow what someone does for me to respond in anger, that gives the person control over how I feel. I'm learning that I am the only one that can control how I feel about any situation in life. The best advice that I was ever given in a meeting, "would you rather be right all the time or at peace?". That one phrase helped me begin to let people be who they are. I can only accept them for who they are. That doesn't mean that I condone their behavior, just means that I accept that I cannot change anyone else,

I can only change my reactions and attitudes towards them. This brought much peace to my life.

I looked up the definition of struggle a couple of years ago and it made so much more sense to me:

Make forceful or violent efforts to get fee of restraint or constriction.

I was controlled by sin my entire life and breaking free of the sinful nature is kind of like that, a forceful or violent effort to be free of sin.

I was just reminded of an experience I had in church, around 2004-05. I began attending church again briefly. One Sunday during a church service, I felt called to the alter. While down there, the minister was praying over me and my body was shaking violently. I had no control over my body at that time. I didn't understand it then, but I do now. Whatever was inside of me was fighting hard against Jesus calling me. The sin was violently opposing Jesus calling me which caused my body to shake violently and uncontrollably. I did not surrender that day. I allowed fear and internal voices, "you're not worthy" to keep from surrendering to Jesus calling me that Sunday morning. I was still trapped in my mind.

I cannot say that I have fully surrendered because I still find myself doing things my way, but God always seems to get me back on track.

August 2021, I went to work for chick fil a. I loved working there, but it began affecting my body badly. Arthritis was kicking my butt. I usually don't have too many problems with my arthritis, but this hard work was causing my body much agony. I stayed and worked through pain many days. I would come home dragging from work, exhausted and in pain.

November 3, 2021, I resigned. I realized that morning that I had put a job before what called me to do. First and foremost, to finish this book. God has been calling me to get involved with church and community as well, which I haven't truly stepped into yet. I'm unsure of the capacity that God wants me to serve in, but I have faith that he'll lead me. Also, I was just elected on the Town Council of our small town. I realized that for change to take place one must be part of the change. I'm not very sure what my calling is there, but God will use me how he wants to use me.

I fully believe that God uses our pain for his purpose, to push us back into his will and out of ours. God didn't tell me to go work at Chic fil a, I chose to do that. It's almost like God was saying, go ahead and do life your way, see what happens. God always says, come to me and I will give you peace and rest. Chic fil a is not a place of rest and you will stay busy, which is not a bad thing. I would recommend that everyone should work there at least once. It is an awesome company to work for and you don't have time to be overthinking about life. It taught me about teamwork. Everyone has their own position and when working together, things always went smoother.

Identity

Genesis 1:27(NLT)

So God created human beings in his own image. In the image of God he created them; male and female he created them.

Genesis 3:6(kjv)

And when the woman saw that the tree was good for food, and that it was pleasant to the eyes, and a tree to be desired to make one wise, she took of the fruit thereof, and did eat, and gave also unto her husband with her; and he did eat.

Genesis 3:7(kjv)

And the eyes of them both were opened, and they knew that they were naked; and they sewed fig leaves together and made themselves aprons.

Genesis 3:11(kjv)

And he (God) said, Who told thee that thou wast naked? Hast thou eaten of the tree, whereof I commanded thee that thou shouldest not eat?

Genesis 3:21(kjv)

Unto Adam also and to his wife did the Lord God make coats of skins, and clothed them.

My interpretation only. Right or wrong, it's how I interpreted these passages.

God is spirit. God created Adam and Eve in his image, which would be the image of spirit. (naked; truth; pure, clean, undisguised). Adam and Eve disobeyed by sinning, they tried hiding their sins from God by blaming the other. God punished them and separated their spirit from him by skin. The skin is a covering to the spirit within each of us. The flesh is sinful, the spirit of God is truth and goodness. With different skins, we in human flesh judge each other, compare ourselves to each other, don't get to know each other because we're too busy judging the outside of the person. When you wake up to God's spirit inside of you, you begin to see things differently. You begin to see with your heart and not your eyes. It doesn't matter what the outside covering looks like, we're all the same on the inside.

I know exactly why I had that interpretation. I was struggling with vanity. Whatever I'm struggling with, God's words will speak to me to help me learn, grow, and change into who he originally created me to be.

Matthew 7:1-2(NLT)

"Do not judge others, and you will not be judged. For you will be treated as you treat others. The standard you use in judging is the standard by which you will be judged".

God created me just the way he wanted to create me. He gave me the skin he wanted me to have. He gave me the height that he wanted me to have. He formed me in my mother's womb. He knew every hair on my head before I was born.

Growing up, I didn't like me. I didn't like my shape, my size, my nose, my looks, nothing about me did I like. This was in total disagreement with what God created. So what did I do? I began to distort God's creation. As I got older, I began to change the way I dressed, the way I acted, in order to fit in or feel accepted by others. I changed myself to be who I thought others wanted me to be or who I thought I wanted to be. Having no clue, mind you, what others thought at all. I never learned to just be myself. I didn't like being different. I wanted to be anyone else but me. This led to misery with myself, abusive relationships, alcoholism, addictions, anything to keep me from feeling anything at all. Through changing myself so many different times, and disagreeing with who God created, I lost my identity of who God had originally created.

What I did was pervert what God had created for good. I allowed sin to control me throughout my life because of being in total disagreement with God and by never being true to myself as an individual. My identity was found in people, places, and things. I felt like nothing when I didn't have someone to be around or something to fill a void. I couldn't stand being with myself long enough to get to know the true me. I was a runner all of my life too. I ran from everything that went wrong, but wherever I went, there I was. It wasn't until I went to recovery that I realized that I was the common denominator in every single one of my problems in life. I was the one with the problem and my problem was me. There is an inner self that will tell you, "hey, you shouldn't do that", but another part of you (ego) that says, "well, I'm going to do it anyway", knowing that what you are about to do is going to end badly. There is a constant battle inside every single one of us that is fighting for us to wake up to truth and not the fantasy that we try and create for ourselves. The ego is fighting against the spirit. The spirit is good and only wants good for you. The ego will say, "I know better" and will do whatever it pleases.

When I was in the middle of evaluating my life, I was at a point where I could see an identity crisis, I took a break. I looked up and said, "God, I'm tired of seeing all of this bad stuff about me. Please show me something good".

I randomly opened the bible to 1 Peter 2 and read it all. What stuck out to me was 1 Peter 2:10(NLT) "Once you had no identity as a people, now you are God's people. Once you received no mercy, now you have received God's mercy."

That's what it says today when I read it. But the first time I read it, I could have sworn it said something a bit different. I thought I had written down somewhere what I read the first time, but evidently I didn't. I thought it said, "you are now a child of God". Basically that's what that says, but I thought those were the exact words I read.

Nonetheless, there was my identity. My identity is found only in Christ who saved me from myself, my sinful being. I literally cried when I read it and thanked and praised God.

Feelings

Feelings are not always facts. A feeling can come from reflecting on memories, good or bad. They come from things people say or do to you. They come from life's experiences. But are they truth? I allowed my feelings to control me for many years and for those many years, my feelings were negative, angry, hateful, etc. Because my feelings changed so much, so did my actions, relationships, jobs, homes, etc.

What do I mean about feelings not always facts? I can give quite a few examples of this. With my 1st marriage, I FELT like my husband was cheating on me. I don't know if it were fact or not. But because I FELT like he was, my feelings guided me right into the arms of another man.

Many times I FELT like I was overlooked or insignificant. Were these feelings facts? No, because I was the one withdrawing from people so it was actually me causing myself to feel that way.

I FELT unloved for most of my life because I didn't get what I wanted the way I wanted things to be or thought they should be. Was this an actual fact? Not really, because, to be able to receive love, one must first give it. I had no love for myself, I hated myself. How could I possibly accept love when I didn't even like me. How could I possibly give what I didn't have? I couldn't. So again, I caused that to myself.

I could sit and think about things from my past that truly hurt me and I would feel those same feelings over and over again. It was a fact that some things caused me pain, but it was unforgiveness that kept me replaying those things in my head. No matter how much I replayed traumas in my head, I had to finally come to the conclusion, that those things were not happening anymore, it was my mind that replayed them keeping me locked in misery. It was just feelings that kept me reacting on situations from years prior that had no business being in the today.

I'm not saying that our feelings aren't real or valid. I'm just stating that feelings come from things we experience and our personal interpretation of the experience, good or bad. Two people could go through the exact same experience and each of them could experience totally different feelings from the exact events. This is why we should never tell others that their feelings are wrong, they're just different than ours. We are "individuals", separate from each other, with our own unique sense of being and feeling. We all have the same feelings and emotions, we just feel differently about different things and that doesn't make one right and the other wrong. What connects us together is being able to empathize with others feelings.

Have you ever been so excited to share a truly great experience with someone else and you're so excited and want them to feel what you feel? Well, they will never be able to feel what you feel. They can be happy for you, be excited for you, but will not be able to feel what you're feeling. This goes the same with bad feelings. When we feel bad, we want others to be able to feel that as well, but it's just impossible. We often don't understand why people just don't feel the same way we do and when we try and make others feel what we're feeling, this leads to control of another.

When we're hurt by someone, we want them to hurt like we do, so we retaliate instead of discussing how something made us feel. Many times we tell our friends what someone did that hurt our feelings. We want others to join us in our anger towards the one that hurt us. We want others to justify us in our thinking and retaliation. This creates more harm than good because when we share with our friends how we were hurt, we don't always share the entire truth, like what our part was in the entire situation. We only tend to cast blame on others so we feel justified in our actions. The better way to handle things is by discussing true feelings with each other without placing blame. We're good about not discussing feelings with each other. We tend to only discuss the actions that hurt us, not the why or how we feel. This leads to blaming and shaming the other. When we decide to open up to each other and discuss the feeling, without pointing out the action, we will find it easier to forgive, heal from it, and move on in life.

If I'm hurt by something someone did, and I only tell them what they did, they are going to have no clue why I am mad or upset with them. Why? Because their intentions may have been totally different than how I interpreted the action itself. Pointing out and saying that what someone did was just wrong to you and being angry and vindictive towards that person, will only create a greater division between the two. A better way of handling these types of situations would be, "hey, can we talk about this? What you said (or did) caused me to feel this way". Then discuss why you feel that way. Ask what they actually meant when saying those things or acting that way to better understand instead of automatically reacting in anger without an understanding of what the other is meaning.

There is a lack of communication in relationships today. Especially with technology that we have. The biggest problem with communication is not listening to comprehend what one is saying before responding. We tend to create a response before we even let the other person finish talking. This is called talking at each other instead of with each other. It takes much practice to be able to listen to someone without forming a response before they finish talking. The more you practice this, the closer you will grow together instead of creating more division with the automatic negative responses.

Unconditional Love

1 Corinthians 13:4-7

Love is patient, love is kind. It does not envy, it does not boast, it is not proud. It does not dishonor others, it is not self-seeking. It is not easily angered, it keeps no record of wrongs. Love does not delight in evil but rejoices with the truth. It always protects, always trusts, always hopes, always perseveres.

When I read this in early recovery, I finally understood it. I understood it early, but did not begin to apply it to myself until much later. I heard it many times in life but truly never read it to understand it or even apply it to my life. I have learned to place my name in these sentences and if they are not true with my name in them, then I must change my attitude, actions, reactions, etc.

I found a prayer book that I wrote two prayers in, April 27th and April 28th of 2021, just before moving back home to my parents in May.

The first one:

April 27th Heavenly Father,

Today, I pray to be united with a "chosen" man. (meaning one that God has chosen for me) One that I can feel your love through. One that I can trust through you. One that understands that he and I will become one with you.

Thank you God for preparing me for this man and preparing this man for me.

April 28th Heavenly Father,

I pray that when you unite your chosen man with me, that he will be able to feel your love and trust through me. I pray that he and I will always come to you in prayer, always giving you the glory for our lives.

I don't remember the exact date because I didn't write it down in my journal, sometime in July 2021, my mom told me that I should hang out with a certain man named Mike, because he and I were both single. I grew up knowing of Mike, we went to the same church, but I didn't remember much about him, only his name. I was totally against it. I was judging him without even knowing him (judgement prior to investigation). I thought of every excuse not to talk with him. Why? Because in my mind, if I were going to be around any man, it was going to be a man of my choice, but in truth, I was waiting for God to send me a man. Do you see the ironic battle there? A man of "my choosing" but waiting for God to send me who he chose. It took a few weeks, but I finally asked him if he wanted to go to Cornerstone with me to watch the series, The Chosen. God had chosen a man for me and was placing him right in front of me, answering my prayers from April.

I wasn't very open to this friendship in the beginning. It was basically me doing my mom a favor by taking Mike with me to church on Wednesday nights to watch an amazing bible series. It was right in front of my face, "The Chosen". He has since attended every one of those nights with me, that I have gone. We have been going to church together on Sundays. We have been to the movies, out to dinner quite a few times, spent hours just talking, and recently attended the State fair. That was a lot of fun.

It is now late October 2021, and lo and behold, feelings popped up within me that I wasn't expecting and surely didn't know what to do with them. I held onto those feelings for a very short while and then decided to express the feelings in words that wouldn't be forcing anything other than a friendship because I know where he is right now in his spiritual journey. I expressed that I had become very fond of him and his reply was the same for me, but he has many fears due to past relationships and I understand fear well. This is where I began to learn more about myself and what love truly means. Love is not of a physical nature or of feelings. Love is not lustful. Feelings come and go, so I cannot rely on feelings or act on those feelings. I must rely on truth and facts. Fact number one, he's not ready for a relationship. Fact number two, he, like myself, has fears due to past pains. Fact number three, nothing can be forced. Forcing anything is only met with resistance and then failure. Force pushes it away from you.

For the last two and a half years, I have learned much patience in life and I believe that God was teaching me to be patient for this very moment in time. Accepting the friendship that I have now and being patient and not trying to force anything more. I must allow life to unfold as it may. If one tries to force a bloom on a flower open, the blooms just break apart. That's just like any relationship, if you force it, it will break apart. This is where I realized that Love is patient. My "self" doesn't always want to be patient though and I have to will that patience into existence with God's help. I have to remind myself all the time, that what I have right now is actually a relationship with Mike, it's called a friendship. Relationship is defined as how one relates to another. I haven't had any negative feelings or any bad moments with Mike since we've been friends. It is just a continual growth forward.

Love is kind. I have learned to be kind to others. Sometimes things I say or do could offend someone else and if that happens, I'm grateful for them telling me so I can look at things from their perspective and learn from that moment to change the way I approach things. In my eyes, I'm always kind to others, but to others, their interpretation could be different.

Love is not easily angered. A week or so ago, Mike told me in the afternoon that he would text me later that night, but he didn't. I got a little upset about that. I know, silly, but that is truth. I thought about it and talked with God about it. My old self would have probably gotten into my feelings about this and allowed those feelings to fester and said something ugly to him or getting angry with him for not following through with what he said he was going to do. While thinking over those feelings and talking with God about them, I realized that Mike could have been busy, he could have gone to bed early, anything could have distracted him, so I let those negative feelings go. You know what happened, he texted me the next day and told me what happened and he had gone to sleep early due to a very busy day. Because I didn't blame him for anything and didn't get angry, I was able to let silly negative feelings go, an underserved confrontation was totally avoided. Being sober minded, I'm able to think more clearly and not be so selfish or self-seeking.

Love does not dishonor others. If I allowed feelings to stew and get angry, that could lead to calling someone out of their name, saying things that I didn't truly mean and not honoring how they may feel about what I would be doing to them.

Love is trusting. I never trusted myself or anyone else for that matter. I have total trust with Mike, only because I trust God. God is not going to steer me in the wrong direction. God brought Mike to me, so I have no reasons to not trust him. He has done nothing to me for me to have any mistrust for him. I no longer filter my past through today. What I mean by this is that I don't look at current situations and look back through my memories for similar ones and rationalizing that if a certain person did this to me in this same type of situation in the past, then Mike would do the same thing to me in the present moment. Those are just lies your mind tells you. Mike is not the person in my past. Mike is different. He is not toxic. I can never judge someone in my present by past pains of what someone else may have done to me.

Love does not envy. When I first began having feelings for Mike, a little jealousy popped up in me. I couldn't believe that I felt that way. It was weird, I haven't felt jealous in awhile, but I had not been close to a man in awhile either. I had to pray to God about those feelings and let them go. They do not belong in love.

Love does not rejoice in evil. Well, I can tell you that for many years, all I knew was pretty evil and I boasted about it. There was no love in me then. Today I am full of God's love and able to share God's love with others.

I have learned to be what I've been learning. Actively living God's words. God continues to work on me because I'm far from perfect, but I'm grateful for where I am in life today.

Love always has hope and always perseveres. When I gave up hope on myself, I was just struggling to survive in life. I failed at everything because anytime something entered my life that was difficult, I quit. Today, I don't quit on life, I continue walking forward, even through difficult times because God is always with me.

The end of October, Mike and I were flirting over text messages. Innocent enough. I had to be honest with him though. I was never honest about my true feelings in the past but have since learned that honesty is the only way to be. I explained to him that it bothered me that he only wanted to be friends, no relationship, but we discussed relational things and were flirting with each other. I'm grateful that I can be honest about my true feelings these days and express them in words. His response to my concerns freed me from my fears. He told me that these past few months of being around each other have affected him in a good way and that he had missed being with someone. He said we could discuss the relationship path. It's good to discuss things before just jumping into them. We should all be able to discuss our personal concerns, what we expect from each other, goals, dreams, how we plan to address problems when they arise, because problems do occur in life, how we plan to grow in God's love together, boundaries due to past trauma for both of us, and whatever is of concern to either of us. If you just jump into a relationship without first discussing these things, you'll have a difficult time understanding each other. You cannot just jump into something expecting someone to know what you're thinking. If you create these expectations of "they should know what I'm thinking" or "they should know what I'm feeling", you're setting yourself up for disappointment. We all need to learn how to comprehend what someone else is saying and listen to their feelings, not denying things they say that we may have done to hurt them. Denial of hurting someone is only justification for actions of self.

New feelings showed up in me. Jealous feelings of Mike's memories. He shares his memories with me. The problem is that when you're in memories, you're not in the present moments of life. I want him to be in the present moments with me and not in his memories, but that's where patience comes into play. We all heal at different times and stages. Besides, he is extremely patient with me and my current fears.

God has taught me so much about myself and life over the past three and a half years and he's been preparing me for this season of my life, a life shared with Mike, a wonderful friendship. Where it leads, only God knows.

I went through a rough spell of thinking, "well maybe this is the guy that God is sending me", I thought that about several different men throughout these past few years. Most of those thoughts quickly left me as I was able to look for the fruits of the Spirit within these men I was looking at.

These are silly, but God knew how to get my attention with Mike. For a few years, I've felt that Archangel Michael has been my guardian angel. I was given a small catholic medallion in active addiction that someone that I barely knew told me to wear for safety. I wore that all the time. It had Archangel Michael on one side and Mary on the other. So, when I began talking with Mike (Michael), I thought, hmmmmm, maybe he is the one God is sending me. Then a few weeks after talking with him, I saw the ring he wears, it is of the tree of life. I had just been giving a necklace by a good friend that has the tree of life on it. With these two little signs, I began looking for the fruits of the Spirit within Mike. He is kind, patient, giving, loving, forgiving, gracious, honest, trustworthy........everything I ever dreamed of in a man. I know that I cannot force anything with him, although the more I am around him, the greater my feelings grow. After I wrote this, I did try and force this relationship several steps ahead of where we should have stayed. I almost messed it up. Thank God for forgiveness.

I accept Mike as he is. I don't try and change anyone for my benefit anymore. People are just people. Only God can change someone.

I've felt at peace with Mike since we've been doing things together. That is a good feeling. If I'm not at peace being around someone, then that is a tell-tale sign that either two people shouldn't be together or that God is continuing to rebuild them and they're just not ready for the next step into the relationship yet.

Love is not something that you just "fall" into. Love is something that you grow into.

The most important thing I've learned about love is that God's love is unconditional. Human love places conditions on each other. God had to restore me and continues to create me his way for me to be able to share his unconditional love with others.

I cannot judge anyone. I cannot hold resentments towards anyone. I must always forgive and let things go. I must be true to myself about what I want and what God wants for me. I cannot be jealous and I must trust and be trustworthy. If I have any of those negative feelings or actions in me towards others, that is not love, only conditions on love. God's love shines through us when we're free from all those things. When I give God control over my life and allow life to happen as it may, it's beautiful. Maybe not always easy, but oh so much easier than how I used to live.

If you find yourself angry all the time with people around you, first check yourself. If you're right with God (not being right with yourself, but with God), look at the people you are surrounding yourself with. I walked away from about 150 people that I had known because I choose not to live life in a bar or on drugs anymore. I choose not to surround myself with people who do those things still because they're toxic to my spiritual connection with God. I'm not saying that a few drinks for some is a bad thing and I could be around that occasionally if at a wedding or family function. I'm referring to those that still live in the bars, party all the time, do drugs, etc. I'm not judging them, because that was my life for a long time, too long. I just know that my life is different today. I pray every night for those struggling to break free from those addictions. The first step is admitting the problem. Underneath alcohol and/or drugs is a lifetime of guilt, shame, resentments, and anger. Just removing the substance is only the beginning of the healing.

God has been providing for me my entire life. I just couldn't see it for a very long time. Now that I recognize God, I recognize what he sends to me or asks me to do for him. It's not always immediate, but I do recognize it eventually. God has been restoring what I messed up trying to live life my way. I'm grateful for each new day. I'm accepting of what I have today and I have to remind myself at times to live in the "right now" and no longer living in wanting what I don't yet have. Patience!!!

Just a couple of days ago, I realized that I can also get in the way of life unfolding how it should unfold. How? Fear. Fear of taking the next step. Life is all about learning and growing and finding that balance with God leading. We tend to fear each other, but with God there is no fear. Fear is just a liar that will keep you stuck until you're willing to grow into the season you're given.

Today, November 3rd, 2021, as I was reading over my prayer book, something clicked and finally made sense that completes a bond and keeps it sacred.

Love is patient. I must be patient with God as he is patient with me. I also must be patient with myself. Love is kind. I must always be kind to God as he is kind to me and I must be kind to myself. Love does not envy. I must never be envious of God as he is not envious of me. Love doesn't keep a record of wrongs. God doesn't keep a record of my wrongs when I repent, and I must never hold God responsible for anything that I do or someone else does that's wrong. I must never keep a record of my wrongs either. Love never lies. God never lies to me, so I must never lie to him and I must be true to myself. Love is not angry. God is not angry with me, so I must never be angry with him and I must not get angry with myself. Love is trusting. I must trust God and I must be trustworthy to God and to myself. God is forgiving, therefore, I also must be forgiving and learn to continue forgiving myself as I am far from perfect. This made me realize that if I cannot keep this covenant with God or myself, then I will never be able to keep this covenant with another person. I must always have God's help and strength to lead and guide me. I must always have reverent respect for God. Everything I give to God is what I give to others. God is love.

I was fearing love, but I realized that I am no longer who I was. I make less of those bad decisions as I did in the past. If I said that I made no bad decisions, then I'd be lying. I just learn from them and move on. I am able to trust myself again when I am true to me. I am able to love me again. I am able to forgive myself when I mess up. I am learning to be patient with myself. I'm slowly letting go of me and becoming who God originally intended me to be, a free loving Spirit.

This journey is not over and I look forward to what God has in store. I had to take a few steps back because I was trying to create life a bit faster than God was bringing it to me. This almost caused great damage, but I gave this to God for him to fix, not me. Anytime I try and fix what I messed up, I end up making a bigger mess.

Now I need to explain why this could have ended badly. I pray when you read this, you'll understand why I had to write this in here. Mike and I went out together as friends and then dated for a total of 6 months. We had already developed feelings for each other and had taken a few steps into a deeper relationship. This is very important! When you're dating someone, you need to share with each other (before taking steps into intimacy) things that you aren't very pleased with about yourself. I'm not talking about just skimming over the issues, but explaining weak areas in each other's lives. Some things were not fully discussed and after they were brought into the light, we took some steps back. I'm not going to place any blame on neither of us, or maybe both of us.

When you're dating someone, each need to be fully open and honest about self. If you leave details out, this will mislead each other while making decisions on whether or not to proceed into a deeper commitment. It's not fair to each other. What happens is that you develop feelings, thinking everything is great, take a few more steps and then boom!! After committing, you begin finding out things about each other that you don't like. Some of the things, that if known early on in getting to know each other, could have changed the choices that were made to begin with. This makes taking steps backward very difficult, but this could have been totally avoided if each one had been completely honest in the beginning and not just trying to put on an impressive face to gain approval from the other.

God is the great redeemer and restorer! If God chooses to restore, he will. Restoration begins with self. If I want something and find that there are things in the way of what I want, like things that consume my thoughts and time, I have to decide what is truly important and give up the rest. I cannot tell anyone else what they need to do, I can only let go of things that no longer have a place in my present life. The longer I take to decide what I choose to do in correcting myself, the further away I put myself from those close to me. It is all in my decision. If I choose not to give things up, I may lose what it is that God is trying to give me. I learned that in order to receive better, I must give up things that I have now. It's not people that leave me or hurt me, it's me doing it to myself by not doing the things that I know I need to do. It's me being closed off to others. It would be my fault for not receiving help when offered because it wasn't the kind of help I wanted, although it may have been the help that God was sending. God doesn't appease our wants, he meets our needs. We only need to accept what's given. We are to want what God wants for us and it's sometimes difficult seeing what that is and then when we do see it, it can be difficult accepting.

I pray that this book helps you find some peace and hope. God is always there, we only need to be quiet and listen.

About the Author:

Paige Jeffcoat, 51 years old, was born and raised on the outskirts of a very small town, North, South Carolina. Yes, that is the name of the town. She grew up in the country with her parents, that just celebrated 58 years of marriage and her two brothers. She is the middle child and only girl. She grew up a tomboy playing in the mud, woods, climbing trees, hunting and fishing. She had a "girly" side as well as she enjoyed playing with her barbies.

At the age of 18, she walked away from church and found herself walking on a path straight to hell. She suffered through 30 years of alcoholism, depression, and addictions. There were several suicide attempts seeking to be released from the pain she felt throughout life. She had lost all hope for a better future and had accepted defeat over alcohol and drugs. At the age of 48, she decided to ask for the right kind of help and went to a recovery center, she had finally been given the gift of desperation.

Paige has 4 wonderful adult children and 8 grandchildren with another one on the way. She has returned to her hometown church, North United Methodist Church in hopes of bringing new growth and life into the church. Although, she returned to this church, she is not religious, she's spiritual and has found the connection with God that she was missing in her life. She found that God is not religious. Jesus is not religious. It is only sin that separates one from a true connection between oneself and a relationship with the Father.

Paige was just elected for a seat on the Town Council of North, South Carolina and has a heart of wanting to help others. For change to happen, one must be part of the change. Change and growth requires action not just wishing for things to be different.

She also continues to mentor females in recovery. She gives back what she's been freely given; love, grace, and mercy. As a Christian believer, she's found that one can only lead by example. I pray this helps those like me find the freedom that I found.

Recovery Intake picture 2018
A mere 94lbs.

Paige today, free from all substance
and living a happy, healthy life.

www.ingramcontent.com/pod-product-compliance
Lightning Source LLC
Chambersburg PA
CBHW020423130626
46549CB00006B/2706